What's Love Got To Do with It?

What's Love Got to do with It?

How the Heart of God Shapes Worship

Sam Hamstra, Jr.

Foreword by
John D. Witvliet

WIPF & STOCK · Eugene, Oregon

WHAT'S LOVE GOT TO DO WITH IT?
How the Heart of God Shapes Worship

Copyright © 2016 Sam Hamstra, Jr.. All rights reserved. Except for brief quotations in critical publications or reviews, no part of this book may be reproduced in any manner without prior written permission from the publisher. Write: Permissions, Wipf and Stock Publishers, 199 W. 8th Ave., Suite 3, Eugene, OR 97401.

Wipf & Stock
An Imprint of Wipf and Stock Publishers
199 W. 8th Ave., Suite 3
Eugene, OR 97401

www.wipfandstock.com

PAPERBACK ISBN: 978-1-4982-8056-3
HARDCOVER ISBN: 978-1-4982-8058-7
EBOOK ISBN: 978-1-4982-8057-0

Manufactured in the U.S.A.

"What's Love Got To Do With It
Words and Musc by Terry Britten and Graham Lyle
Lyrics Used by permission
© 1984 WB MUSIC CORP. and SONGS OF KOBALT MUSIC PUBLISHING
All Rights Reserved

"Seven Stanzas at Easter" from TELEPHONE POLES AND OTHER POEMS by John Updike, copyright © 1958, 1959, 1960, 1961, 1962, 1963 by John Updike. Used by permission of Alfred
A. Knopf, an imprint of the Knopf Doubleday Publishing Group, a division of Penguin Random
House LLC. All rights reserved.

CONTENTS

Foreword by John D. Witvliet | vii
Preface | xi
Acknowledgments | xv

1. Introduction | 1
2. The Beloved Whom We Worship | 17
3. How the Beloved Shapes the Person Who Worships | 34
4. How the Beloved Shapes the People Who Worship | 53
5. How the Beloved Shapes the Practices of Worship | 77
6. How the Beloved Shapes the Context of Worship | 95
7. How the Beloved Shapes the Music of Worship | 121
8. Conclusion | 138

Bibliography | 143
Author index | 149
Scripture index | 151
Subject Index | 155

FOREWORD

I LOVE BOOKS LIKE this—books that emerge when someone like Sam Hamstra thinks prayerfully about the students who will walk into his seminary course on worship, and what he is most eager to convey to them. There is such a rich reservoir of wisdom to draw from, from Sam's years of thoughtful engagement as a Bible reader, pastor, historian, theologian, musician, teacher, and disciple of Jesus. There are so many disciplines to draw from: biblical theology, systematic theology, the history of worship, cultural anthropology, musicology, and more. There are so many practices to describe: prayer and preaching, baptism and the Lord's Supper, testimony and fellowship, music and architecture, and more. There are so many errors to warn students about: individualism and narcissism, moralism and Deism, and more. There are so many excellencies to embrace: God-centeredness and winsome orthodoxy, hospitality and faithful witness, and more.

Yet there are also profound constraints: only six chapters, only two hundred pages, only a semester of class sessions. There is only so much that can be said of all the good things that could be said. And ultimately, what will matter most over time is not the discussion of a long list of particular techniques or strategies, but rather something deeper—a way of perceiving God and the world God loves, a set of pastoral dispositions and attitudes that will help students grow in their capacity to love God and to exercise leadership in ways that earn trust and foster reliance on the life-giving work of the Holy Spirit.

A volume like this emerges then out of a crucible of abundance and constraint. Such is the nature of a genuinely pastoral theology.

Like all the best books in pastoral theology, this one is a fusion experiment. It is shaped by insights from Biblical exegesis and by personal experiences, and sharpened by insights and turns of phrase from cultural icons, ethnomusicologists, philosophers, and other pastoral leaders. As the book unfolds, we get to know the author, with vignettes from Professor Hamstra's own life as husband and father, son and grandson, teacher and pastor. The list of Bible texts that inform the book speak to a life of Bible study in both Testaments, with insights from both Leviticus and Revelation, both the Psalms and Romans, both I Samuel and the gospel of John. The footnotes offer a fascinating record of Sam's reading and exploration through the landscape of historic and contemporary Christianity: Calvin, Edwards, and Nevin; Barth and Bonhoeffer; Hagemen, Horton, Farley, Old; Webber and Hybels.

Like all the best books in pastoral theology, this one commends a Spirit-shaped growth-mindset by modeling it. Among the passages that particularly struck me were those in which Professor Hamstra reflected on past gaps and mistakes, and resolved to change—to emphasize mutual love more, to not avoid doctrinal catechesis and church's distinctive theological vocabulary. This kind of self-revealing candor gives us a sense of learning that is still unfolding. It creates anticipation in us about what the Holy Spirit may lead each of us to better understand and know in the years to come.

Like all the best books in pastoral theology, this one is not only the result of prayerful discernment; it also invites students to engage in continuing discernment. Indeed, one of the underlying themes of the book is the challenge that churches of all kinds face in discerning the difference between enduring transcultural practices and appropriate ways of contextualizing worship given the dynamic interplay of cultures that converge in any given congregation. We live in a period of remarkable dynamism and change—that kind of time that can be both energizing and unnerving, leaving even the most vigorous innovators a bit queasy. In this context, I am so grateful for the calm, poised way that Sam returns again and again to say that it the triune God who orients and invites us, who corrects and challenges us, who enables and perfects our worship. There is no other foundation or anchor or source of poise for us than the very being of the triune God.

Like all the best books in pastoral theology, this one is marked by a distinctive gospel-shaped tone of voice. So much of what we read and hear in the world today is marked by fear of getting it wrong, or by a sentimental yearning, or by a breathless quest to live on the cutting edge of innovation, or by a cynically critical dismissal of the bold, old, and new. Fear, sentimentality, ungrounded enthusiasm, and cynicism gain force as they take over our ways of speaking to each other—our fundamental "tone of voice." In contrast, the tone here is warm, poised, winsome, and compelling. It is a tone shaped by the theme of other-centered love that weaves through nearly every page. Even if some students forget some of the details within each chapter, I pray that they will never forget to emulate this tone. For an emphasis on mutual love is not just a cognitive theological claim; it is a way of being, something that shapes not only what we think, but what we feel and desire, and how we habitually talk together about the deepest matters of faith.

Finally, like all the best books in pastoral theology, the ideal audience for this book is much larger than only those who might take a seminary course on worship. While the courses Professor Hamstra teaches may be designed for emerging congregational leaders, this book is of great potential value for all worshipers—whether new to the faith or lifelong believers. This is a wise book to study together in community, and to read, even in small doses, each week before going to church. Participation in worship is such a profoundly counter-cultural activity. Very few activities in our common life are analogous to it, and it often takes a while to adjust to the particular kinds of self-giving love that worship invites us into. There are many ways that congregations can invite people to prepare their hearts for worship. But one good one would be for congregations to invite individuals or families or small groups to read paragraphs from this book as a weekly discipline of preparation. May God's Spirit use this book to encourage and strengthen many worshipers in joyful, faithful, loving communion with God and each other.

John D. Witvliet
Calvin Institute of Christian Worship
Calvin College and Calvin Theological Seminary
Grand Rapids, Michigan

PREFACE

FOR EIGHTEEN MONTHS I enjoyed the privilege of participating in a colloquy on Reformed worship sponsored by the Institute of Reformed Theology at Union Theological Seminary and Presbyterian School of Christian Education (Union-PSCE). It provided a splendid opportunity to talk about worship with about thirty Reformed Christians from throughout the United States of America. This group of scholars included pastors, professors, and church professionals from the Presbyterian Church (USA), the Reformed Church in America, and the Christian Reformed Church in North America. We met on five occasions over two years, including three times on the campus of Calvin College, and once each on the campuses of Hope College in Holland, Michigan, and at Union-PSCE in Richmond, Virginia.

During our final session we touched on the "great divide" between theory and practice. In preparation for that meeting, I attempted to identify principles which shape the weekly gatherings of God's people, otherwise referred to as corporate worship or Sunday services. I submitted a document to my peers for their review. That document led to the publication of *Principled Worship* (Wipf & Stock, 2006), the forerunner to this volume. In *Principled Worship* I affirm that the weekly gatherings of God's people will be shaped or regulated by something or someone. I then suggest that our weekly gatherings best be shaped by biblical principles. On that foundation I identify and comment upon biblical principles that, to one degree or another, shape the weekly gatherings of God's people. In time, I recognized the deficiencies of that volume, the most obvious of which was the absence of love. So, I began reworking it, focusing on the formative power of love, into, what I hope, is a better treatment of that which regulates corporate worship.

You may ask, "Why another book on worship?" Or, "Can anything be added to the deep pool of knowledge created by countless reflections on the subject?" But could it be that, in spite of the multitude of books on worship, something has been overlooked? That the most important aspect of worship has not even been addressed? That no one has asked, "What's love got to do with it?" Amazingly, during the past thirty or so years American Protestants have covered *ad nauseum* nearly every aspect of worship but one. We have read about seeker-sensitive worship, emerging worship, blended worship, as well as worship styles, worship evangelism, and worship arts. We have explored ancient worship, the history of worship, worship wars, planning worship, leading worship, and the prayers of worship. But who has asked this question: What's love got to do with it? This book asks and answers that question, believing that the answer to that question is more important than the answer to any other question.

During the last three decades, a significant conversation has been taking place among Americans about corporate worship. While the conversation includes several tangents, including, but not limited to music, spiritual formation, technology, and visual art, at the center has been a discussion on the factors which shape the corporate worship of local congregations. The Seeker-Sensitive Movement, led by Bill Hybels, proposed that the weekly gathering be shaped by the unchurched.[1] The Ancient-Future Movement, led by the late Robert Webber, countered by highlighting the formative role of ancient tradition.[2] A third group, led by biblical theologians, has asserted that corporate worship be shaped by Scripture.[3] Still another group approaches corporate worship with an overarching narrative or theme in mind; much like a systematic theologian, these

---

1. See, as examples, Strobel and Hybels, *Inside the Mind of Unchurched Harry and Mary*, and Dobson, *Starting a Seeker Sensitive Service*.

2. From Robert Webber's many excellent publications on the subject, see *Ancient-Future Worship* and *Worship Old and New*.

3 See, as examples, Carson, *Worship by the Book*, Cherry, *A Blueprint for Designing Culturally Relevant and Biblically Faithful Services*, Peterson, *Engaging with God*, and Ross, *Recalling the Hope of Glory*.

authors employ a theme as a thread to connect the variety of biblical teachings on corporate worship.[4]

I enter that conversation with this publication. Like each of the aforementioned groups, I approach the conversation with the acknowledgment that something or someone will shape the weekly gatherings of God's people. In summary, I assert that the core of the Christian life is summarized in two commandments: to love God with all our heart, soul, mind, and strength, and to love our neighbor as ourselves. I then assert that the entire Christian life—including corporate worship—must be understood as a loving response to our Triune God's love. Finally, I assert that since love is determined by the Beloved, not the lover, we must go to the Scriptures to learn the heart of God so that we may love him with our worship. Ironically and surprisingly, during the last three decades of intense conversation about corporate worship, no author has addressed the vital link between love and worship, this in spite of the apostle Paul's clear teaching that corporate worship is null and void without it. So, like the third group, my approach to worship is founded upon biblical principles and, like the fourth, I employ a thread to connect the variety of biblical teachings on the subject.

The primary audience for this book is pastors, worship leaders, liturgists, congregational leaders who oversee corporate worship, Christian college teachers, and students preparing for Christian ministry. The book will also be of interest to students of Christian spirituality and corporate spiritual formation, as well as to individuals or small groups exploring the subject of worship. It will also be of interest to any Christ-follower who recognizes that the heart and soul of the Christian life is love—God's love for us and our love for God and neighbor—and God's love for us and our loving response to the love of God has everything to do with worship.

In my Introduction, I establish my thesis that worship represents the loving response of individuals and congregations to the love of the Triune God, our Beloved. More importantly, I assert that the shape of the lover's love is determined by the beloved, not by the lover. When we apply this principle to worship, we must conclude that our Triune God—our Beloved—determines what constitutes an appropriate loving response to his love. In the chapters that follow, I describe how the heart of our Triune God shapes corporate worship, beginning with a description of

---

4. Representatives of this group include: Chapell, *Christ-Centered Worship*, Horton, *A Better Way*, Quicke, *Preaching as Worship*, and Morgenthaler, *Worship Evangelism*.

how God the Father calls us to worship, God the Son Mediates our worship, and God the Holy Spirit empowers our worship (Chapter 1). Then I explore how our Beloved has shaped and continues to shape us for worship by creating us in his image so that we long, even need to worship, but need to do so authentically (Chapter 2). In the next chapter I explore how our Beloved shapes the congregation that gathers for worship; I delineate how congregations have been called and formed to worship as a loving, unified, chosen, visible, baptized, and diverse people. In the next three chapters I address how the heart of our Triune God shapes the external aspects of worship. I describe how the love of our Triune God prompts transcultural practices—praise, prayer, confession, gift giving, discipline, and recollection—that have been experienced for centuries by those who love the Lord and which, in the process, have helped worshipers become better lovers and better worshipers (Chapter 4). I explore the subject of inculturation (the context for worship), more specifically, the tension between worship and four aspects of culture: language, space, aesthetics, and technology (Chapter 5). In Chapter 6, with help from the field of ethnomusicology, I address the prevalence, power, function, types, and styles of music. In the conclusion, I summarize my argument that corporate worship is our loving response to the love of the Triune God, our Beloved, and then invite the reader to commit to congregational worship shaped by the heart of God. This invitation will include the acknowledgment that, too often, we have worshiped something other than our Triune God, approached worship as individual consumers, found it convenient to limit worship to preferred practices, and failed to recognize the corrupting influence of culture. In short, we have failed to love our Beloved.

ACKNOWLEDGMENTS

I RELEASE THIS PUBLICATION with gratitude to many. I begin with thanks for the Rev. Dr. John Witvliet, director of the Calvin Institute of Christian Worship. Back in the autumn of 2002, while I was serving as pastor of the Palos Heights (IL) Christian Reformed Church, he invited me to participate in a two year conversation on worship with thirty people from three denominations. His invitation, and the subsequent conversation, fueled the fire in my belly about corporate worship.

I give thanks for the Rev. Dr. Charles Hambric-Stowe, the former Academic Dean of Northern Seminary in Lombard, Illinois. In 2007, he was faced with the horrible news that the beloved Dr. Robert Webber, the late William R., and Geraldyn B. Myers, professor of ministry at Northern Seminary, would not have the health and strength to teach his scheduled course on worship. He asked if I would step in. I did with much fear and trepidation, openly acknowledging my inability to approximate in any measure the knowledge and wisdom of Dr. Webber. I have been teaching courses on worship at Northern Seminary ever since—and I am still not measuring up to my predecessor.

I give thanks to the students of Northern Baptist Theological Seminary in Lombard where I have had the privilege of teaching since 2007. Together, we have explored our biblical theologies of worship, the history of worship, the future of worship, multi-cultural worship, everything in our weekly liturgies but sermon and song, and how to plan and lead worship. Together we have reviewed and edited the earlier drafts of this publication. Most significantly, together we have worshiped our Triune God. During each experience, we have enjoyed our sevenfold unity as brothers and sisters in Christ: one body, one Spirit, one call, one Lord, one faith, one baptism, and one God and Father of all, who is over all and through all and in all (Eph 4:4-6).

I give thanks to the congregations I have had the privilege of serving as pastor and worship leader since 1980. Each congregation has granted me the privilege of planning and leading corporate worship. Each one affirmed my conviction that the weekly gathering of a congregation lives and breathes the interplay between a particular gathered community, the culture in which it lives, and, above all, the prompting of our Triune God. Each has blessed me more than I could ever bless them. Each, I add as a matter of disclosure, was a Reformed congregation that self-described itself as Evangelical and that preferred semi-formed but mostly free liturgies. All but one was WASP, by which I mean White-American-Suburban-Protestant.

Finally, I give thanks to Debbie, my bride of forty plus years, and our children and grandchildren. They embody our Triune God's wonderful grace to me and a perpetual reason for thanksgiving.

chapter 1

INTRODUCTION

BACK IN 1984 TINA Turner recorded her Grammy Award Winning song "What's Love Got to Do with It?"[1] It was #1 on the pop music charts for three weeks—in spite of its somewhat cynical message. The lyrics, written by Terry Britten and Graham Hamilton Lyle, raise suspicion about the motivating force which draws a man and woman together:

> You must understand
> Though the touch of your hand makes my pulse react
> That it's only the thrill
> A boy meeting girl
> Opposites attract
>
> It's physical
> Only logical
> You must try to ignore that it means more than that
>
> Oh what's love got to do got to do with it?
> What's love but a second-hand emotion?[2]

I was drawn to Tina Turner's classic song as a title for this volume because, over the last fifteen years of study, I have discovered that

---

1. In 1985 *What's Love Got to Do with It* won three Grammy Awards: Record of the Year, Song of the Year, and Best Female Pop Vocal Performance. In 2012 the song was inducted into the Grammy Hall of Fame.

2. "What's Love Got To Do With It?" Words and Music by Terry Britten and Graham Lyle. Used by permission. © 1984 WB Music Corp. and Songs of Kobalt Music Publishing. All Rights Reserved Alfred Music.

the majority of contemporary white, American, suburban Protestant (WASP) Christians, and perhaps others, seem to have concluded that love doesn't have much to do with worship. I have been drawn to that conclusion because, over the past few decades, countless books and blogs have been written about worship with seldom a word about the essential role of love.

Compare that reality with the apostle Paul's teaching to the first-century church in Corinth, a congregation that enjoyed the outpouring of the Holy Spirit in their individual lives and spectacular manifestations of that same Spirit during their gatherings. The Holy Spirit allowed some, like those blessed on the day of Pentecost, to speak the language of the Holy Spirit and so confirm his presence among them. The Holy Spirit empowered others with faith like that of the apostles to lead the persecuted church with hope and confidence through the dark nights of persecution. The Holy Spirit empowered others to speak the Word of God with power to an infant church in need of direction. The Holy Spirit even encouraged some to sacrifice themselves for the advancement of the Gospel.

The apostle Paul challenged the congregation's preoccupation with the spectacular gifts of the Holy Spirit and accused them of neglecting the greatest gift of all: love. He shared the lyrics of a hymn that describes love as the greatest spiritual gift because all others are ineffective without it. Through this poem we discover that love is the greatest spiritual gift because the extraordinary gifts of the Spirit are ineffective without love. It is the greatest because love is the root from which all fruit grows. It is the greatest because, unlike the spectacular gifts of the Spirit, love is eternal; it never fails. Passionate preaching, excellent music, sound liturgies, sacrificial service, generous contributions, solid doctrine, and numerically growing congregations are wonderful blessings, but "the ordinary influence of the Spirit of God, working the grace of love in our hearts, is a more excellent blessing than any of the extraordinary gifts of the Spirit."[3]

For that reason alone, love is the best place from which to begin a conversation about the worship of our Triune God. We continue the conversation by linking Paul's teaching on love with Jesus' summary of the Christian life in Matthew 22. There we read that Jesus calls us to lives of love for our Triune God and for our neighbors (37–39). In other words, love is the heart and soul of the Christian life and, subsequently, the heart

---

3. Edwards, *Charity and Its Fruits*, 30.

and soul of worship. But there is more. Worship is our loving response to the love of our Triune God, the ultimate lover of our souls. We have been loved by God the Father who has extended grace to us in Jesus Christ and who draws us to himself by the power of the Holy Spirit. Ideally, then, our worship flows from hearts touched by love. We desire to respond to the amazing love of our Triune God with loving acts of devotion, one of which is our worship, both personal and corporate. At least that is our hope, lest it be said that we come near to the Lord with our mouths and honor the Lord with our lips while our hearts are far from him (Isa 29:13).

Love of the Lover Shaped by the Beloved

How shall we lovingly worship the Lord, our Beloved? Here's a simple answer to that question: love is determined by the beloved, not the lover. When a young man "falls in love," his heart filled with awe, he spontaneously expresses love for his beloved through words or actions. Not wanting to convey the wrong impression, he initiates an investigation. He talks to friends and family members of his beloved to learn her longings, preferences, and desires. It would be disastrous, for example, to offer her a box of chocolate if she is a diabetic; such a gift could be interpreted as anything but love. During the course of his research the young man discovers that his beloved enjoys roses. So, after a trip to a money machine, he picks up and delivers a dozen beautiful flowers. The response of the beloved is everything he had hoped for.

That illustration from the everyday lives of lovers affirms that the beloved determines whether or not a gift from the lover constitutes love. The beloved, not the lover, determines if an action is a loving act. Regardless of the lover's motives or intent, the beloved will decide if an action amounts to love. When we apply this principle to our loving response to our Triune God's love, *we are reminded that our Beloved—our Triune God—will determine how we worship*. Regardless of our motives or intent, our beloved determines if our acts of devotion amount to love. A story from the life of David affirms this thesis. In II Samuel 6 we read,

> David again brought together all the able young men of Israel—thirty thousand. He and all his men went to Baalah in Judah to bring up from there the ark of God, which is called by the Name, the name of the Lord Almighty, who is enthroned between the

cherubim on the ark. They set the ark of God on a new cart and brought it from the house of Abinadab, which was on the hill. Uzzah and Ahio, sons of Abinadab, were guiding the new cart with the ark of God on it, and Ahio was walking in front of it. David and all Israel were celebrating with all their might before the Lord, with castanets, harps, lyres, timbrels, sistrums and cymbals. When they came to the threshing floor of Nakon, Uzzah reached out and took hold of the ark of God, because the oxen stumbled. The Lord's anger burned against Uzzah because of his irreverent act; therefore God struck him down, and he died there beside the ark of God. Then David was angry because the Lord's wrath had broken out against Uzzah, and to this day that place is called Perez Uzzah. David was afraid of the Lord that day and said, "How can the ark of the Lord ever come to me?" He was not willing to take the ark of the Lord to be with him in the City of David. Instead, he took it to the house of Obed-Edom the Gittite. The ark of the Lord remained in the house of Obed-Edom the Gittite for three months, and the Lord blessed him and his entire household.

In that story we find two lovers of God loving the Lord by delivering the Ark of the Covenant to Jerusalem. In preparation, Uzzah and Ahio secured a new cart, one without defect. They placed the Ark of the Covenant on the cart. They connected two oxen to the cart and began their journey to the city of David. On the way, the oxen stumbled, the cart shook, and it appeared as though the ark might fall to the ground. It was then that Uzzah reached out and stabilized the ark on the cart. A loving act for sure. Right? But apparently the Lord did not think so. In verse 7 we read, "The Lord's anger burned against Uzzah because of his irreverent act; therefore God struck him down, and he died there beside the ark of God." When I read that story I am confused by God's seemingly harsh judgment but also reminded that the Beloved, not the lover, determines whether an action constitutes love. Uzzah may have thought his action loving, but the Lord thought otherwise.

Is it not irrefutable, then, that the beloved shapes the forms by which the lover expresses affection? By that assertion I do not wish to imply that the beloved, at all times, accurately interprets the actions of his or her lover. A child, while still feeling the pain of a parent's discipline, may, at that moment, view his beloved's action as anything but love. Nevertheless, in time, that same child will reflect on his mother's action and see it for what it was intended to be: the love of a mother for her son. The same could be said of an adult whose family intervenes with the hope that their beloved would be set free from a destructive addiction. At the moment of the intervention, the addict may view her family's treatment as malicious and selfish but once on the side of freedom, she views it as a courageous act of love.

With those exceptions in mind, may we agree that the beloved shapes the love of the lover? May we also affirm that if worship represents our loving response to our Triune God's amazing love, then our Triune God—our Beloved—shall determine or shape how we worship? It seems appropriate, if not indeed necessary, then, to view personal and corporate worship *as attempts by lovers (followers of Jesus) to love (acts of worship) the Beloved (our Triune God.)* This principle seems so self-evident that it need not be stated. Yet, a cursory review of the countless books on worship published over the last few decades betray scant attention to love. While the Jesus we follow teaches that love is to characterize every action, discussions on worship seldom call worshipers to love. While the apostle Paul shocks us with his teaching that the absence of love makes null and void even the post spectacular worship practices, discussions on worship tend to neglect even an introductory comment regarding the importance of love.

Here then is my basic premise: worship is an act of love by devoted followers of Jesus, and the shape of this act is to be determined, not by the lover, but by our Beloved, the Triune God. Furthermore, since our Beloved determines whether or not our forms of worship constitute love, it seems equally appropriate for us as lovers to know God's heart and mind concerning worship. So, before we introduce a new practice or ritual into our personal worship or into the weekly gathering of God's people, we best ask, "Will our Triune God view this as an act of love?" That simple question will steer us through the many options we face each week. In fact, how we answer that question may not be as important as simply asking the question. After all, love is determined by the Beloved, not the lover.

Worship and Word

Since the beloved shapes the love of the lover, the starting place for our discussion of how we worship our Triune God, begins with our Triune God. Since we hope that our forms of adoration will constitute loving acts of devotion, we seek to discover God's preferences for worship. After all, what we think may be a loving act, such as stabilizing an ark on a cart, may be viewed by God as an irreverent act. Plus, Scripture testifies with one voice that worship is serious business: both sons of Eli, Nadab and Abihu, as well as Korah's party, suffered death for offenses relating to improper worship practices (1 Sam 2; Lev 10; Num 16).

The best place to discover our Triune God's preferences for worship is the written Word of God. There we discover that our Triune God cares deeply about how we express our love to him through worship. The first four words in the *Ten Commandments* (Exod 20:1–11), for example, speak directly to worship. There we discover prohibitions against worshiping other gods, graven images, and taking the Lord's name in vain. When we move on to the book of *Leviticus* we discover a divinely prescribed annual calendar of festivals and sacrifices. In the *Psalms* we discover the place of song in worship, and in the Prophets, the place of obedience (Isa 58). Through the teaching ministry of Jesus we discover God's preference that our gifts for the poor be offered and received without public acknowledgment. In the words of Jesus, we are "not to let our left hand know what our right hand is doing" (Matt 6:1–4). In the letters of the apostle Paul we learn that acts of worship, even extraordinary ones like speaking in tongues or prophecy, are invalid if not motivated by love. Throughout the *New Testament* we discover the radical impact of the New Covenant upon the worship of God's people. In addition, through a study of the history of God's people we see them, time and time again, falling short of God's design for worship; yet we also find God, time and time again, forgiving, renewing, and restoring them to their place his beloved:

> Thus says the LORD: In this place of which you say, "It is a waste without human beings or animals," in the towns of Judah and the streets of Jerusalem that are desolate, without inhabitants, human or animal, there shall once more be heard 11the voice of mirth and the voice of gladness, the voice of the bridegroom and the voice of the bride, the voices of those who sing, as they bring thank offerings to the house of the LORD: "Give thanks to the LORD of hosts, for the LORD is good, for his steadfast love endures forever!" For I will restore the fortunes of the land as at first, says the LORD (Jer 33:10–11).

Interestingly, while searching through the Scriptures for God's preferences for worship, we do not find a prescribed form of worship. We don't discover one liturgy for God's people. We don't uncover one way, valid at all times and in all places, to worship the Lord. In fact, we learn that worship by God's people changes from one period to another. In the absence of one authoritative method, we conclude that there must not be one way of loving God through worship, "nor can there ever be."[4] But that's not the end of our search. We have been called as a particular people to love God in a particular place and at a particular time. So we continue our search and discover that, while the Scriptures do not provide a permanent order of worship for God's people, they include principles that reflect the God's preferences for our worship. As such, they serve as guides to our corporate response to the grace of God. Our work towards loving worship, then, is not trying to recapture the past by uncovering a biblical directory of worship for God's people at all times.[5] Instead, by discovering principles of worship from Scripture, we allow our Beloved to shape our worship here and now, as well as the future.

The Regulative Principle

This approach to the practice of worship echoes the conviction of the sixteenth-century Protestant Reformers who advanced a position now labeled "the regulative principle." This position was articulated by John Calvin and his followers, as well as by the sixteenth-century Puritans during their lively debates with the Church of England. Elsie McKee describes the two versions of the regulative principle. "All the Reformers agreed that nothing in worship may contradict Scripture, and some went further and made Scripture the paradigm for right worship."[6] Michael Farley refers to these two versions as the theologically-orientated regulative principle and the praxis-orientated regulative principle.[7]

The praxis-orientated regulative principle was and is held by many in the Calvinist (Reformed and Presbyterian) wing of the Protestant Reformation. This version asserts that, even with biblical principles in hand, Christians should only worship in a manner which has direct sanction from God's Word. In other words, if a practice is not recorded in Scripture, we should not do it; we should not ask of ourselves or of God's

---

4. Hageman, *Pulpit and Table*, 124.
5. Aumann, *Christian Spirituality*, 10.
6. McKee, "Reformed Worship," 8.
7. Farley, "What is 'Biblical Worship'?," 592–96.

people anything that does not have explicit scriptural warrant. In support of this view, the Westminster Confession states the following:

> The light of nature shows that there is a God, who has lordship and sovereignty over all, is good, and does good unto all, and is therefore to be feared, loved, praised, called upon, trusted in, and served, with all the heart, and with all the soul, and with all the might. But the acceptable way of worshipping the true God is instituted by Himself, and so limited by His own revealed will, that He may not be worshipped according to the imaginations and devices of men, or the suggestions of Satan, under any visible representation, or any other way not prescribed in the holy Scripture. (XXI.1)

Faithful to that historic confession, Edmund Clowney writes, "The church has authority to order worship, but not to introduce new elements beyond those that God has provided." He adds, "The church, in its rightful sphere of authority, may order worship. But ordering worship activities that the Lord approves is not the same as adding those that he has not approved, especially since participation in public worship is not optional."[8]

The theologically-orientated regulative principle follows the conviction that the Bible does not contain an order for worship, a comprehensive directory for worship, or parameters for worship practice in every time and place. Instead, it offers historical precedents and theological principles which shall shape the worship of God's people to such an extent that no aspect of worship contradicts the will of God. Lukas Vischer writes,

> In Scripture we encounter a community responding to the living God, and we are called to associate ourselves to this response. The pattern of the response will not at all times and places be the same. God meets us where we are, and we respond out of our particular situation; and always and everywhere, God is present and speaks to us through word and sacrament, in the community of faith, and we—the gathered community—communicate with God in prayer.[9]

Currently, there are two models of the theologically orientated regulative principle: the patristic–ecumenical and the biblical–typological.[10]

---

8. Clowney, *The Church*, 120–23.
9. Vischer, *Christian Worship*, 282.
10. Farley, "What is 'Biblical Worship?,'" 596–601.

Those who have adopted the patristic–ecumenical model, such as Geoffrey Wainwright, Alexander Schmemann, Simon Chan, and Robert Webber, develop their liturgical theology in the following manner: First, they derive biblical support for worship practices "not only by looking for New Testament commands and examples but also by evaluating the way that particular practices embody biblical truth, even if such practices are not explicitly attested in the New Testament;" second, they rely almost exclusively on the "New Testament for their biblical foundations;" and third, "they draw their ideals for liturgical practice from post-biblical liturgies, especially liturgies form the patristic era as well as the ecumenical liturgical consensus about the Eucharistic *ordo* that emerged in the twentieth-century liturgical movements (both Catholic and Protestant), which sought to recover ancient liturgical models from the era of the undivided church."[11]

Proponents of the biblical-typological model of the theologically orientated version of the regulative principle, most-notably Allen Ross and David Peterson, take a different approach.[12] Whereas the praxis-orientated version and the patristic-ecumenical model focus most of their attention on the New Testament, the biblical-typological model draws upon both the Old and New Testaments as it searches for God's preferences for worship. "By reading the Old Testament with a typological lens, they seek to derive normative principles and patterns of practice from the Old Testament that can shape Christian liturgy when suitably translated into forms appropriate for the new covenant community."[13] This explains why some refer to this approach as the normative principle of worship. Furthermore, "they largely embrace and value the same post-biblical liturgies esteemed by the patristic-ecumenical group. However, they devote much more attention to finding biblical warrant for those liturgical patterns and developments in the Old Testament, and they are more willing to critique and adapt those post-biblical liturgies on the basis of their biblical theology of worship."[14]

Now it is time for disclosure. In this volume, I have adopted the biblical-typological model of the theologically-orientated version of the regulative principle. I can think of four reasons for this decision. First, like

---

11. Ibid., 597.
12. Ross, *Recalling the Hope of Glory*, and Peterson, *Engaging with God*.
13. Farley, "What is 'Biblical Worship'?," 602.
14. Ibid.

the other options, it prescribes an important role for Scripture. Second, it affirms, more than the others, that worship shall be shaped by the heart of God, not just by the rites and rituals found in Scripture, any of which can be practiced without love. Of course, every practice can become rote but by insisting that our worship practices reflect the heart of God we may, by way of association, teach worshipers that the worship we practice reflect our hearts. Third, it grants the Holy Spirit an active role in shaping the worship of the gathered community. In order to know the heart of God for worship, we must live by the Spirit and spend time in the Word. The combination of Spirit and Word within a specific, local gathered community provides the essential ingredients for an exciting and dynamic environment which is being reformed according to the heart and will of God. Finally, I find that while the logic of the praxis-orientated version is internally consistent, so is that of the theologically-orientated approach. Clearly, the Bible does not provide a liturgy or detailed instructions for conducting worship, but it does confirm, over and over again, that our Triune God (our Beloved) shapes the worship (love) of his people (the lovers). For that reason, we must diligently seek to know the heart of God for worship. We may do so with the help of the Holy Spirit who promises to guide us into truth and within the context of the one, holy, catholic, and apostolic church. With the Spirit within us and the church surrounding us, we may study the Scriptures in search of biblical and theological principles to shape our worship. When we apply those discoveries to our worship, each of our liturgical actions will have biblical support and nothing in worship will contradict Scripture.

The task which remains, then, and the focus of this book, is to identify the biblical principles which shape the worship of our Beloved and, thereby, serve as guides to our loving response to the "gracious and redeeming act of God in Jesus Christ."[15] This means that "while one cannot point to a single liturgy and say that it contains the only form of genuine worship, some are clearly better than others."[16] They are better for one simple reason: love is shaped by the beloved, not the lover.

---

15. Horton, *A Better Way*, 142.
16. Ibid.

Concluding Matters (Definitions)

Before proceeding through a review of the biblical principles which reflect God's preferences for our worship, I offer clarification on the words liturgy and worship. If you are an "Evangelical," you may not like the term "liturgy."[17] It "may seem like a dirty word . . . suggesting the Roman Catholic mass or the Episcopalian prayer book, accompanied by vestments, candles, and altars."[18] But the term "liturgy" could have more play in the Protestant Church, especially among Evangelicals. The word derives from the Greek λειτουργια, transliterated as *leitourgia*, a word that means "public work" or the "work of the people." Jordon Aumann notes that, when used in its traditional Greek sense, the word refers to "the public service rendered by an individual to the community."[19] Frank Senn notes that in the Greek Old Testament (Septuagint), "the word *leitourgia* was used to translate the service rendered by the priests in the temple," that this use is seen in the New Testament with reference to the service rendered by Zechariah (Luke 1:23) and by Jesus Christ (Heb 8:6), and that, in Acts 13:2, *leitourgia* is used with reference to the worship of the church.[20]

The word "liturgy," then, may simply refer to one act of public service or to the collection of components within a ceremony, ritual, or service. You could use the word, for example, to refer to the rituals which accompany a Major League Baseball game. The liturgy of the game includes rituals like throwing out the first pitch, the national anthem, a pre-game conference with the umpires, the introduction of the starting line-ups, the game itself, and the seventh-inning stretch. Like a baseball game, every gathered community of Christ-followers follows a liturgy. As one denominational report states, "Every church has a liturgy, whether it worships with set forms inherited from the ages or whether it worships in the freedom of the moment. The only question is whether we have the best possible liturgy: it is never whether we have a liturgy."[21]

---

17. With David Bebbington, I understand an "Evangelical" Christian congregation or organization as one characterized by Biblicism, crucicentrism, conversionism, and activism. See his *Evangelicalism in Modern Britain*.
18. Hart & Muether, *With Reverence and Awe*, 92.
19. Aumann, *Christian Spirituality*, 27.
20. Senn, *Introduction to Christian Liturgy*, 5.
21. From the "Liturgical Committee Report," *Acts of Synod of the Christian Reformed Church*, 135–36.

In this work, I use the word "liturgy" in its broadest yet simplest application: to refer to the work of the people that make worship possible. The liturgy provides the framework within which we worship our Triune God. Most important for this discussion, I propose that we consider liturgy as a broader concept than worship. For sure, just as a ball game prompts the creation of a liturgy, so worship prompts the creation of a liturgy. Worship is the core of the liturgy but—and this is a big exception—the liturgy properly includes elements which we do not usually consider acts of corporate worship. In other words, it includes our coming and going. It includes what we do once we are together, including our ritual partaking of coffee and cookies or the weekly litany of announcements regarding our life together. Frank Senn writes,

> Liturgy can thus refer to a public and well–defined ritual. It is often translated as "ministry" or "worship" in English-language Bibles. But there is a difference between "liturgy" and "worship" in that worship suggests the honor and praise accorded God communally or individually, in the public assembly or in worldly activity, whereas liturgy suggests something that is done communally and publicly, or is at least communal and public in derivation even if it is a ministration extended to those absent from the assembly.[22]

The distinction between liturgy and worship begs for a definition of the latter. As a teacher of worship to the next generation of pastors and worship leaders, I have had the privilege of discovering and analyzing many definitions of worship. James White has been a great help in that process.[23] He has observed three typical methods by which students and scholars clarify what they mean by "Christian worship." First, some look at the key words used to describe the corporate weekly gathering of God's people. One such word is *worship*. Linguists have analyzed the word in its original context and believe it is a compound word deriving from two Anglo–Saxon words: *worth* and *ship*. These linguists then tell us that the simple meaning of that word is to declare the worth of someone or something. Frank Senn adds,

> In its older sense in English of worthiness or respect (Anglo-Saxon, *worthscripe*), worship may on occasion refer to an attitude toward someone of immensely elevated social status, such

---

22. Senn, *Introduction to the Christian Liturgy*, 5.
23. White, *Introduction to Christian Worship*.

as a lord or a monarch, or, more loosely, toward an individual, such as a hero or one's lover. Magistrates in England are still addressed "your worship." In the old *Book of Common Prayer*, at the exchange of rings in the marriage service the groom said to his bride, "with my body I thee worship." In this sense worship means "respect" or "serve."[24]

Linguists, of course, don't really define words; they simply demonstrate how they may have been used in a particular context. Furthermore, the meaning of a word typically follows its usage, which means that dictionaries are more often than not descriptive, not prescriptive. For this reason the unique context of a writer must also be factored into the equation. When we do that, we realize that one word may have multiple meanings, a reality which leads to some uncertainty, if not outright confusion.

Second, some think the best way to understand worship is to describe it rather than define it. So they look at what Christians do when they gather for worship and describe those practices. More specifically, researchers in this camp survey the liturgies of the weekly gatherings of God's people throughout the centuries to discern the constants within the diversity. Wherever you find these constants, then, you may conclude that you have found worship. In this group we find Robert Webber who identified the constant of this fourfold movement of the liturgy: Gathering–Word–Thanksgiving–Dismissal. In the same vein, Donald Bloesch identified these four constants: Praise–Proclamation–Recollection–Prayer. Simon Chan opted for two: Word–Sacrament. Clearly, that approach typically leads to a broad understanding of worship, one often framed by Paul's teaching that all of life is to be our act of worship (Rom 12:1). One is left, then, explaining how each act of the liturgy describes the worth of our Triune God. Once again, the work of Frank Senn is helpful here:

> The Greek New Testament word for worship is *latreia*, "to serve." Paul uses this word in Romans 9:4 to refer to the sacrificial rites instituted by God in the old covenant. Likewise, in Hebrews 9:1,6, the term is applied to the official service of the priest in the temple. But in Romans 12:1 *latreia* is expressed in the "living sacrifice" of their bodies with which Christians serve God. Thus Paul views the entire activity of Christians as service to God.[25]

---

24. Senn, *Introduction to the Christian Liturgy*, 4.
25. Ibid.

White's third approach is to check out the definitions of others. When we do so, we find concise summaries of what Christians do when they gather each Lord's Day. James Torrance offers this definition: "Worship is the gift of participating through the Spirit in the incarnate Son's communion with the Father."[26] New Testament scholar Ralph Martin writes that worship is the "dramatic celebration of God in his supreme worth in such a manner that his worthiness becomes the norm and inspiration of human living."[27] D. William Temple opines that "to worship is to quicken the conscience by the holiness of God, to feed the mind with the truth of God, to purge the imagination by the beauty of God, to open the heart to the love of God, and to devote the will to the purpose of God.[28] Welton Geddy offers a definition appropriate for this book: "worship is a gift between lovers who keep on giving to each other."[29] The most popular model for defining worship is as a twofold action of God's grace or initiative and humanity's gratitude or response. There are several variations of this model. Peter Brunner writes, "God gives himself to us and that self-giving prompts our response." John Piper writes, "worship is a way of reflecting back to God the radiance of his worth."[30] Robert Webber, in a book written near the end of a remarkable career as a theologian, defined worship in this way: "Christian spirituality is God's passionate embrace of us; our passionate embrace of God."[31] In a similar fashion, Donald Bloesch writes, "worship is a creative response to God's gracious act of condescension in Jesus Christ."[32] Simon Chan goes with worship as "the church's response to God's initiative in revealing who he is."[33] John Burkhart defines worship as the "celebrative response to what God has done, is doing, and will do."[34] When all is said and done, I wonder if Franklin Segler offers the best observation: "Christian worship defies definition; it can only be experienced."[35]

---

26. Torrance, *Worship*, 30.
27. Martin, *The Worship of God*, 4.
28. Temple, *The Hope of a New World*, 30.
29. Geddy, *The Gift of Worship*, xi.
30. Piper, *Desiring God*, 84.
31. Webber, *Divine Embrace*, 16.
32. Bloesch, *Church*, 119.
33. Chan, *Liturgical Theology*, 52-53.
34. Burkhart, *Worship*, 17.
35. Segler, *Understanding Christian Worship*, 7.

As tempting as it may be to let that last statement draw me away from defining worship, a book on worship requires a definition of the word. In this project, I have chosen to define worship narrowly, as those loving acts by which we honor, adore, praise, and glorify our Triune God for who he is and what he has done for us. This worship takes place corporately and privately, in the sanctuary and on the streets, on Sunday and throughout the week. But to that definition I add another, one founded upon its broader usage in the Old Testament, where the Hebrew word for worship may be translated as service (as in Exod 3:12, for one example). Worship is that which Christians do when they gather each week. It is the Sunday service or liturgy in action. So understood, while each action in the liturgy is part of the worship service, each act is not necessarily an act of worship, narrowly understood. In summary, worship narrowly understood is an act or acts by which we honor, adore, and praise our Triune God; worship, broadly understood, is what Christians do when they gather each week. Narrowly understood, worship is part of the Sunday morning service. Broadly understood, worship is the Sunday morning service. You may think such a distinction unnecessary but it helps in two ways. First, it affirms that not every liturgical action is or need be an act of worship whereby we, like the Psalmist, specifically praise our Triune God for his goodness and greatness and grace and more. Second, it distinguishes between our personal acts of worship or adoration of our Triune God, and the Sunday or Worship Service. One is narrow and the other broad—but both are worship.

Finally, this book has been designed for those responsible for planning the weekly worship service of God's people. Built on the conviction that worship is our loving response to the love of our Triune God, and that our loving response shall be determined by the Beloved, not the lovers, this book attempts to discover our Beloved's preferences for worship and, in the process, identify biblical principles which shall shape the worship of our Beloved. It articulates principles that guide the formation of a congregation's liturgical life, that help worship planners discern between the genuine and the spurious, between "what is abiding and what is ephemeral."[36] I hope that the end result will be a congregation whose worship is shaped by the heart of God. Paul Fromont captures what I hope would be the experience of every person or group planning worship:

---

36. Bloesch, *Church*, 139.

> They will creatively stretch outward from the edges. They will preserve the old without resisting the new. They will be characterized by an opening outwards, an unfolding of creative and meaningful new praxis and forms. They will have a firm grasp of their core beliefs and values, and will operate out of a strongly theological framework. Their life will be less about perpetuating trendiness, about being "trendy," and more about integrity, faithfulness, authenticity, and relational depth.[37]

For worship planners to reach such lofty heights, it may be best to read the book within a group setting, rather than in isolation from others, and over a couple months rather than over a couple weeks. Like dinner at a fine restaurant, the book will be more helpful when enjoyed with others and in a leisurely manner.

---

37. Fromont, *Belonging*.

chapter 2

THE BELOVED WHOM WE WORSHIP

Growing up in a traditional church with a rich history of congregational song, I sang many hymns, including "I Sought the Lord and Afterward I Knew." The author of the text remains anonymous but my congregation assumed she was a faithful follower of John Calvin. Regardless of her theological lineage, I hope to meet her someday for I would like her to share with me the story that gave birth to her words. They describe the experience of many who have sought the Lord only to discover that God, the "Hound of Heaven," first pursued them, his beloved.

> I sought the Lord, and afterward I knew
> He moved my soul to seek him, seeking me.
> It was not I that found, O Savior true;
> No, I was found of thee.
>
> Thou didst reach forth thy hand and mine enfold;
> I walked and sank not on the storm-vexed sea.
> 'Twas not so much that I on thee took hold,
> As thou, dear Lord, of me.
>
> I find, I walk, I love, but oh, the whole
> Of love is but my answer, Lord, to thee!
> For thou wert long beforehand with my soul;
> Always thou lovedst me.

Isn't this where worship begins? Is not worship simply our response to God's love to us in Christ? Don't those who have been touched by God's amazing grace long to love the Lord through worship? Our initial attempts at worship don't amount to much more than the best of our broken selves lovingly offered to the Lord. Like a young child with crayons and construction paper creating her first Mother's Day card, we give it our best effort. It isn't pretty, but it is authentic. Inevitably, it falls far short in content and grandeur of the eternal worship taking place in heaven where angels sing perpetual praise, but it is our sincere response to God's grace.

Our response takes many shapes, one not better than the other. For Abraham, worship took the form of the tithe. When young Josiah first began to seek the Lord, he tore down pagan shrines (1 Chr 34). When Moses finally caught some time alone, he wrote a poem and sang a song (Deut 32). When David got excited, even giddy, he danced to the Lord. When the prostitute found the Lord, she kissed and washed his feet (Luke 7:37–39). You may worship the Lord by shouting but one word: "Hallelujah!"

In time, as we experience more of God's grace, mature in the faith, and grow in our love, we discover more about God and, therefore, more about the worship of God. A comparison to Josiah is helpful here. Prompted by the Spirit, Josiah, who became the king of Judah at the age of eight, began to seek the Lord when he was sixteen years old (2 Chr 34:3). A few years later, even without the aid of Scripture, he began reforming the worship of God's people by purifying Jerusalem of its pagan rituals. Then, while in the midst of that activity, Josiah discovered the Law of Moses. After dusting off and reading his new discovery, he continued his reformation by reshaping the worship of God's people in a way that reflected the heart and mind of God.

Similarly, after initially worshiping the Lord, or even while worshiping the Lord, we encounter more and more of God's Word. Through this discovery, we receive a window to the heart and mind of God. Similar to the experience of Josiah, our loving encounter with God's Word reshapes our worship. This doesn't necessarily mean our initial attempts at worship fell short of God's glory. At that time and place, they represented sincere and loving, though uninformed and childlike, responses of faith to the great and glorious grace of God. But now, as a result of our encounter with the Scriptures, they give way to more informed and, we trust, equally loving acts of worship.

As we spend more time in God's Word, we make an incredible discovery. Unlike nearly every other religion (if not every religion), we discover our one living and true God (Deut 6:4) exists in plurality (Gen

1:26). Given more time, we discover that we worship one God in three persons: God the Father, God the Son, and God the Holy Spirit. In other words, we discover that our God is a Triune God. Remarkably, we also discover that each person of the Godhead is related to the others in ways that imply differences. This allows us to distinguish between the persons of the Godhead, realizing that each person fulfills specific functions. So, we learn to refer to our Triune God as Creator, Redeemer, and Sustainer. We learn to thank God the Father for sending his son, to thank God the Son for dying on the cross, and to petition God the Spirit for power and grace. But just when we think we have the persons of the Godhead placed in their proper roles and our relationship to each one figured out, we discover that each member of the Godhead cooperates with the others. It was, for example, God the Father who so loved the world that he sent his son (John 3:16). Still, God the Son cooperated in that mission by accepting his assignment, humbling himself, and taking the form of a servant (Phil 2:7). Likewise, while we would attribute the resurrection of Jesus to God the Father (Acts 2:32), God the Son proclaims that he raised himself (John 10:17–18), and the Holy Spirit lets us know about his role in the process (Rom 1:4). This cooperation between the Father, Son, and Holy Spirit expands our view of our Triune God. On one hand, it hinders us from getting too specific when thinking about the functions and roles of each person of the Godhead. On the other hand, it encourages us to embrace a more fluid understanding of the relationship between the three persons.

All this talk about function and cooperation and persons may seem doctrinaire and disengaged from worship were it not for the fact that our understanding of the Triune God flows not just from Scripture but from experience. What we have come to call the doctrine of the Trinity represents our attempt to understand and describe our experience. We have been saved by a Triune God: God the Father loved us before the foundation of the world, God the Son died for us, and God the Spirit raised our dead souls so that we may come to the Lord in faith. When it comes to salvation, God the Father initiates, God the Son effects, and God the Spirit perfects. Furthermore, as disciples we live each day with our Triune God: God the Father over us, God the Son beside us, and God the Spirit within us. Add to that, we are blessed by a Triune God: the grace of our Lord and Savior, the love of God, and the fellowship of the Holy Spirit (2 Cor 13:14). We even pray because of a Triune God. God the Spirit prompts our prayers (Rom 8), God the Son intercedes on our behalf as our Great High Priest (Heb 4:14–15), and God the Father receives the prayers prompted by the Spirit and mediated by the Son (Heb 4:16). Most importantly for this conversation, we worship a Triune God. In short, God the Father calls us to worship, God the Son mediates our worship, and God the Spirit empowers our worship. In this manner, our Triune God shapes how we worship.

God the Father Calls Us to Worship

For one reason or another, we get out of bed on a Sunday morning and head off to a place called church, where we gather with some people to worship the Lord. From our perspective, it seems like we decide to worship the Lord, but the longer we are at it, the more we begin to understand that God calls us to worship him. So, while it initially appears otherwise, we conclude that our worship begins, not with us, but with God. We reach that conclusion because the Scriptures teach that it is God the Father who created us, in cooperation with God the Son who has redeemed us, and God the Spirit who sustains, calls, or initiates our worship in three ways.

First, God the Father initiates our worship by creating us to worship him. Hughes Oliphant Old succinctly summarizes that truth with these words: "We worship because God created us to worship him. Worship is at the center of our existence, at the heart of our reason for being."[1] The Westminster Shorter Catechism echoes Old's sentiment pronouncing that our purpose as humans, our "chief end," is "to glorify God and enjoy him forever." The apostle Paul argues this point in his letter to the Romans. In Romans 1:18–23, he teaches us that every human being witnesses the invisible qualities of God in creation and should therefore worship him instead of idols. In other words, when we live as God designed us to live, we witness how God's glory shines over all the earth, discover that his love is higher than the heavens, affirm that his faithfulness reaches to the skies, and, for those reasons and more, glorify the Lord. As the Psalmist once sang:

> When I consider your heavens, the work of your fingers, the moon and the stars, which you have set in place, what is man that you are mindful of him, the son of man that you care for him?.. O Lord, our Lord, how majestic is your name in all the earth! (Ps 8:3–4,9)

---

1. Old, *Worship Reformed*, 1.

There is another layer to the truth that God the Father initiates our worship. God the Father, who has created us to worship him, has created us in his image or likeness so that we can worship him (Gen 1:26). Animals, in contradistinction to human beings, cannot worship God. However, because we have been created in the image of God, we may communicate with God, pray to God, and worship God. As Geoffrey Wainright observed, "humankind is seen through Scripture as made by God sufficiently like himself for communication to take place between the Creator and the human creature, a personal exchange in which each partner is meant to find satisfaction.[2] This means, as Thomas Long notes, we don't have to make worship relevant. For human beings created in the image of God, worship is as relevant as bread and water. We have been designed to worship. We want to worship. We need to worship. It is necessary to being human for, as Alexander Schmemann observed, we are "*homo sapiens, homo faber* . . . yes, but, first of all, *homo adorans*."[3] To this point, Long writes,

> When all the clutter is cleared away from our lives, we human beings do not merely need to engage in corporate worship; we truly want to worship in communion with others. All of us know somewhere in our hearts that we are not whole without such worship, and we hunger to engage in that practice. Thus, planners of worship do not make worship meaningful; worship is already meaningful.[4]

Unfortunately, the image of God within us has been distorted and disturbed by sin. So, left to ourselves, we fail to fulfill our purpose of worshiping the Lord in spirit and in truth. In response to our condition, God the Father, in a manner of speaking, recreates us for worship. He does so through the redemptive work of Jesus Christ. A.W. Tozer asks,

> Why did Christ come? Why was he conceived? Why was he born? Why was he crucified? Why did he rise again? Why is he now at the right hand of the Father? The answer to all these questions is, "in order that he might make worshipers out of rebels; in order that he might restore us again to the place of worship we knew when we were first created."[5]

---

2. Wainwright, *Christian Worship*, 9.
3. Schmemann, *For the life of the World*, 15.
4. Long, *Beyond the Worship Wars*, 17.
5. Tozer, "Worship, the Missing Jewel," 217.

Tozer's words affirm those of the apostle Paul who teaches us that the Lord saved us from our sins, adopted us as his children, and indwelt us with the Holy Spirit "to the praise of his glorious grace" (Eph 1:6). Lest we doubt Paul, the apostle Peter echoed his teaching: "You are a people who belong to God, that you may declare the praises of him who called you out of darkness into his wonderful light" (1 Pet 2:9).

God the Father, then, initiates our worship, not only by creating us in his image for that purpose, but by saving us for worship. God invites us to respond to his saving grace in Christ with gratitude. His salvific grace, then, prompts our praise. We witness the dynamic relationship between salvation and worship throughout the Scriptures, but particularly in the narratives surrounding Christ's birth. Each person or angel who heard the message of salvation praised the Lord! Mary sang, "My soul magnifies the Lord and my spirit rejoices in God my Savior" (Luke 1:46–47). An angel of the Lord joined a great company of the heavenly host and praised the Lord (Luke 2:9–12). Astrologers from the East found Jesus and worshiped him (Matt 2:11). Seems safe to conclude that those whom God saves worship him! Walt Wangerin captures that conviction with this prayer:

> O Lord, you are the musician, and we are all your instruments. You breathe, and we come to life. You breathe, and we are horns for your glory. You blow through the winds of the spirit, and we like chimes cannot keep silent. You pluck the strings of our hearts, and we become a psalm. You come, and we must sing.[6]

Even now, we, who have been saved by grace, delight in the presence of our Savior and glory in the beauty of his holiness. Those impulses will remain with us through eternity for in heaven, we, with all the angels and all the saints, will worship the Lord singing, "Praise and glory and wisdom and thanks and honor and power and strength be to our God for ever and ever" (Rev 7:12). Until Christ comes again, sin continues to derail God's plan for us. Our love becomes disordered. It gets aimed at the wrong ends and enjoys the wrong things.[7] Consequently, instead of worshiping the Lord, we worship ourselves. Influenced by the ever-present power of sin, we enjoy the blessings of the created world and the comforts of our redemption while failing to worship God, the giver of

---

6. Wangerin Jr., *Preparing for Jesus*, 82.

7. I am indebted to James K.A. Smith for pointing me to Augustine's description of the effect of sin. See Smith's *Desiring the Kingdom*, 52.

every good and perfect gift. For that reason the Lord has not only created and saved us for worship, he also commands us to worship Him.

Scripture includes numerous commandments regarding worship, many of which may be found in the Psalms. In Psalm 113, for example, we read: "Praise the Lord! Praise the Lord all you peoples! From the rising of the sun to the place where it sets, the name of the Lord is to be praised!" God's mandate corrects any and all self-centered approaches to worship. It reminds us that we don't worship the Lord to have our needs met or to feel better about ourselves or to get something out of it, though each of those objectives may be reached during times of praise. Instead, we worship in obedience to God's Word, regardless of how we feel. We worship the Lord even when it seems like an irrelevant waste of time. Why? Because God the Father calls us to do so. Our response to his grace and mercy is a loving act of obedience to the Father who has loved us in Christ and who lives with us through the Spirit. Consequently, we ought to worship the Lord even if we don't get a thing out of it.

That is seldom the case because we have been created in the image of God to worship the Lord. In other words, we need to worship the Lord and, consequently, find satisfaction and joy through worship. When we worship with God's people we get something out of it. Our needs are met. We feel complete, even happy. When we worship we know a little bit about the Psalmist's claim that a day with the Lord in worship is better than a thousand doing something else. When circumstances hinder us from gathering with God's people for worship, we long for our return. When we contemplate the future, we freely borrow the words of the Psalmist who said, "One thing I ask of the Lord, this is what I seek: that I may dwell in the house of the Lord all the days of my life, to gaze upon the beauty of the Lord and to seek him in his temple" (27:4).

God the Son Mediates Our Worship

God the Father calls us to worship by creating us for worship, recreating us for worship, and by mandating our worship. Still, fear of getting it wrong may hinder us for the Bible reveals a jealous God with strict demands regarding worship. Anxiety rises as our search through God's Word reveals meticulous and divinely prescribed detail for the logistics of worship and definitive divine punishment for those who fail to implement them. The book of Leviticus, for example, paralyzes us with precise rules for a variety of offerings, the role of priests, purification rituals, as well as the appropriate times of the year to offer specific sacrifices. Add to that the violent stories of one or more of God's people, beginning with Cain, who, with the best of intentions, sought to serve or worship the Lord only to fall short of God's will for their lives—and suffered the consequences.

Such stories cultivate an attitude of fear within worshipers but so does the ever-growing awareness of the holiness of God. A.W. Tozer once wrote,

> Holy is the way God is. To be holy He does not conform to a standard. He is that standard. He is absolutely holy with an infinite, incomprehensible fullness of purity that is incapable of being other than it is. Because He is holy, His attributes are holy; that is, whatever we think of as belonging to God must be thought of as holy.[8]

When we witness the glory of God in his holiness we become more aware of our sins and shortcomings. Like Isaiah, we cry "Woe to me!" or "I am ruined! For I am a (person) of unclean lips, and I live among a people of unclean lips, and my eyes have seen the King, the Lord Almighty" (Isa 6:5). With Job we admit that we need someone to smooth out the way between us and the Father: "If only there were someone to mediate between us, someone to bring us together ... Then I would speak up without fear of him, but as it now stands with me, I cannot" (Job 9:33, 35).

The fear generated by our recognition of God's will for our worship and the holiness of God provide the context within which we understand and appreciate the role of Jesus Christ as our mediator. Jesus answers the questions raised by our study of God's Word, particularly our reading of the Law of Moses with all of its rules and regulations. Jesus also diminishes our fear that our worship will, in some form or another, be found lacking by our Triune God. As the book of Hebrews reveals, Jesus completes two very important works with respect to worship. First, Christ fulfills the system of worship prescribed in the Law of Moses by offering himself as a perfect sacrifice to God the Father. He came to this earth to do what we fail to do. As James B. Torrance points out, Christ came "to offer to the Father the worship and the praise we failed to offer, to glorify God by a life of perfect love and obedience, to be the one true servant of

---

8. Tozer, *The Knowledge of the Holy*, 105-6.

the Lord."[9] This benefits us, Torrance continues, because "in worship we offer ourselves to the Father in the name of Christ because he has already in our name made the one true offering to the Father, the offering by which he has sanctified for all time those who come to God by him (Heb 10:19, 14), and because he ever lives to intercede for us in our name."[10]

Second, Christ replaced the system of worship prescribed in the Law of Moses and inaugurated a new day for the worship of God by God's people. Jesus inaugurated a new covenant and replaced "the whole pattern of approach to God prescribed under the Mosaic Covenant."[11] He offers a perfect sacrifice to God the Father, as the atonement for sin, and lives and reigns as our High Priest through whom we have access to God the Father and through whom we may offer our sacrifices of praise. In so doing, Jesus Christ inaugurates a new day for the worship of God's people. Now through Jesus—and only through Jesus—we may offer worship that is pleasing to God. We do so on the coat tails of him who has offered and continues to offer perfect worship to the Father. So, in Hebrews 4:14–16 we read:

> Therefore, since we have a great high priest who has ascended into heaven, Jesus the Son of God, let us hold firmly to the faith we profess. For we do not have a high priest who is unable to empathize with our weaknesses, but we have one who has been tempted in every way, just as we are —yet he did not sin. Let us then approach God's throne of grace with confidence, so that we may receive mercy and find grace to help us in our time of need.

For some time I had been unsettled by discussions about the mediatorial role of Christ in worship. When I first came across the writings of Torrance, Peterson, and others, I felt like they were asking me to stop worshiping Jesus Christ so that I might join Christ in his worship of God the Father. I couldn't harmonize that feeling with the occurrences in Scripture, most prominently in the book of Revelation, where Christ is worshiped. I couldn't harmonize that feeling with witness of the early church, as evidenced, in one example, by Pliny who, in his letter of 111 AD to the emperor Trajan, described the Christians in Bithynia in this way: "They were accustomed to meet on a fixed day before dawn and sing responsively a hymn to Christ as to a god." Finally, I couldn't

---

9. Torrance, *Worship*, 14.
10. Ibid., 50.
11. Peterson, *Engaging With God*, 228.

harmonize that feeling with my personal desire to worship Jesus as my Lord and Savior.

In time, however, I have come to see that, like many who have come before me, I may and should worship God the Son, as well as God the Father and God the Spirit. But I now understand that I may do so—without fear and trembling—only because of the work of Jesus Christ, the mediator of my worship. With him I cry "Abba Father." Without him, no matter how hard I try, my worship will never be received by our Triune God as an act of loving adoration. It will always fall short. So, if I hope to love God through my worship, I must worship in the name of Jesus Christ who offers the Father the worship I am incapable of offering.

A simple illustration has helped me apprehend the mediatorial role of Christ in worship. If worship is the destination appointed by God the Father for every human being, and if God the Holy Spirit is the automobile (with GPS) we drive to reach that destination, then God the Son provides the roads upon which the car travels to its destination. Without that road, we cannot hope to respond to our Triune God's loving grace with adoration and praise. This means that, in the end, the worship of our Triune God is not only prompted by grace, but made possible by grace. It begins and ends with God. It also means that "Jesus Christ is the leader of our worship, the high priest who forgives us our sins and leads us into the holy presence of the Father."[12] Only Christ, can lead us into the presence of the Father. Not our music, not our relics, not our devices, not our traditions, only Christ. And for that reason, and much, much more, I will not only worship God the Father in the name of Jesus Christ, but I will worship Jesus Christ.

God the Spirit Empowers Our Worship

At one time or another, you have been part of a civic, gathered community, a group of people gathered in one room for one particular purpose. Perhaps you had that experience as a member of a Parent Teacher Association (PTA), or as a Veteran of Foreign Wars (VFW), or as a member of a political party. We may have many reasons for participating in those kinds of gatherings, one of which is that we believe they bear a kind of fruit that cannot be produced by isolated individuals. We understand

---

12. Torrance, *Worship*, 57.

that there is a unique power or potential that rises from within a gathered community.

To a casual observer, the weekly gathering of Christians may appear similar in nature to a political rally where partisans display their placards and chant their slogans. But Scripture has a surprise for us. It reveals that the weekly gathering of Christians is far more dynamic and holds far more potential than any gathering of like-minded individuals. It is also far more substantive than the sum of its individual participants. The Church is, in fact, the body of Christ and the temple of the Holy Spirit. As Simon Chan notes, the local church is the presence of Christ made alive by the Holy Spirit.[13]

As the presence of Christ made alive by the Spirit, the church is a charismatic fellowship. First, those who gather have been baptized by the Spirit into the body of Christ (1 Cor 12:13). Furthermore, by that baptism, they have been anointed into the threefold work of Christ as prophets, priests, and kings. Through the work of the Holy Spirit, every believer, as a priest, may confidently approach the throne of grace in prayer (Heb 4:16), every believer, as a prophet, must be prepared to defend the faith, and every believer, as a king, may exercise his or her spiritual gifts and, thereby, extend the reign of Christ in the world. Lesslie Newbigin writes,

> To be in Christ is to share in His anointing, to have that Spirit by whom the word was made flesh and by whom the incarnate Word was anointed that He might fulfill the mission for which He was sent; it is to have "an anointing from the Holy One." And this anointing is nothing doubtful or debatable; on the contrary, it is the sure fact upon which we can rest our confidence that we are in Him and He is us: "Hereby we know that he abideth in us, by the Spirit which he gave us (1 John 3:24)."[14]

But there is more. The apostle Paul assures us that every follower of Jesus is a temple of the Holy Spirit (1 Cor 6:19) and gifted by that same Spirit for service to Christ in the church and world (1 Cor 12:7). The apostle writes, for example, that the Spirit has gifted some as pastors and teachers "so that the body of Christ may be built up until we all reach unity in the faith and in the knowledge of the Son of God and become mature, attaining to the whole measure of the fullness of Christ" (Eph 4:12). The Holy Spirit also empowers believers with gifts of leadership

---

13. Chan, *Liturgical Theology*, 21–40.
14. Newbigin, *The Household of God*, 99.

and encouragement, while gifting others with creative gifts that find fulfillment in the liturgy of God's people. We may conclude, borrowing words from Jean-Jacques Suurmond, that, by the Spirit, Christians are liberated "to become a gift for others in their own specific identity, and thus to make a contribution to the celebration of community life."[15]

But there is still more. The apostle Paul not only teaches that individual believers are temples of the Holy Spirit, he also teaches that "you all"—the gathered community, the church, the local fellowship of believers—are a temple of the Holy Spirit (1 Cor 3:16). This means that when we gather at the invitation of God the Father in the name of Jesus, the Holy Spirit dwells among us. As such, we are a charismatic fellowship gifted by the ever-present Spirit for ministry in the name of Jesus. For this reason we may conclude that our gathering, worship included, is "inspired by the Spirit, empowered by the Spirit, directed by the Spirit, purified by the Spirit, and bears the fruit of the Spirit."[16] It is filled with Pentecostal promise.

And how we need that promise. We gather each week as a broken people, our spiritual senses impaired by sin. Even though we have been born again by the Holy Spirit, we often hear what we want to hear and see what we want to see. Add to that the unfortunate truth that our cold hearts, stubborn wills, and closed minds too often hinder the work of the Spirit in our lives, an action Paul describes as "grieving the Spirit" (Eph 4:30). If we doubt our spiritual limitations, we need but review the tainted history of the Christian church. In our tattered past, we discover professing Christians committing heinous atrocities in the name of the Lord and, were it not for grace, we would do the same.

Aware of our brokenness and limitations, we thank our Triune God for the gift of the Spirit. We realize that, were it not for the Holy Spirit, we could never love the Lord. The Holy Spirit is, as St. John of the Cross (1542–1991) experienced, our "living flame of love" by whom we mount the ladder of love.[17] It is God the Spirit who convicts us of sin and guides us into truth (John 16:5–15), who brings light into our darkness so that we may see the glory of God in the face of Jesus Christ (2 Cor 4:6), who encourages our weary hearts and quenches our thirsty souls. It is God the Spirit who makes it possible for us to pray "Our Father,"

---

15. Suurmond, *Word and Spirit at Play*, 54.
16. Old, *Worship Reformed*, 5.
17. St. John of the Cross, *The Dark Night of the Soul*, Book II, Chapter XIX.

(Rom 8:15). It is God the Spirit who searches our hearts and intercedes on our behalf when we don't know how to pray (Rom 8:26–27). It is God the Spirit who plays an essential role in both preaching (Eph 6:17) and baptism (1 Cor 12:13).

Because of the promised presence of the Holy Spirit, we may gather with God's people expecting nothing less than a meaningful encounter with God or, as Dallas Willard wrote, a "purposive interaction with the grace of God in Christ."[18] John Calvin describes that phenomenon as "a living moment proceeding from the Holy Spirit, where the heart is righteously touched, and the understanding illumined."[19] When we come together, then, with all of our spiritual limitations, we hope that the Holy Spirit—not the preacher or the music or the liturgy—will mysteriously, freely, and unpredictably touch our hearts, minds and wills. Of course, while we may assume the Spirit's presence with the gathered community, we may never presume the Spirit's blessing. The Spirit works freely and sovereignly, blowing where and when he wills. So, even though the Spirit is present with the gathered community, we ask the Holy Spirit to bless us. "Unless the living Spirit Himself takes the things of Christ and shows them to us, we cannot know them."[20]

The question of how the Holy Spirit freely blesses the gathered community has been a subject of intense conversation among Christians for a long time. Many Christians, especially those who describe themselves as Pentecostals or Charismatics, gather each week believing that the Holy Spirit works today as in the first century. With that expectation in mind, they design liturgies that allow for the full expression of spiritual gifts, including prophecy, tongues, interpretation, even prayers for healing.

Another group of Christians, a large one at that, has adopted a distinction between what they refer to as the "ordinary" work of the Spirit and the "extra-ordinary" work of the Spirit. On one hand, this group of Christ-followers gathers weekly expecting the Holy Spirit to work through ordinary means, such as the teaching and preaching of the Word. For them, the ordinary work of the Holy Spirit comprises those gifts that have been linked to human agency, such as preaching, teaching,

18. Willard, *Renovation of the Heart*, 22–23.

19 This quote is from an unpublished translation by Robert Johnson of John Calvin's preface to his 1542 "Form of Prayers and Ecclesiastical Chants with the Manner of Administering the Sacraments and of Solemnizing Marriage According to Customs of the Ancient Church."

20. Newbigin, *The Household of God*, 101.

leadership, encouragement, hospitality, love, and the like. In such cases, the Holy Spirit works through gifted believers who also happen to be temples of the Holy Spirit, and it is very difficult to discern a difference, if there is one, between a person's talents and a person's spiritual gifts. On the other hand, this same group of Christ-followers gathers each week not expecting to witness the "extra-ordinary" gifts of the Holy Spirit, those gifts which seem to work above and beyond human agency, such as prophecy, tongues, interpretation, and healing (1 Cor 12:7–11). They believe, in short, that their time has passed; they have ceased operating. Hence, there is little to no similarity between their weekly gatherings and the type of gathering Paul describes in I Corinthians 14. Abraham Kuyper aptly summarizes that traditional or *cessationist* position with these words:

> The charismata now existing in the Church are those pertaining to the ministry of the Word; the ordinary charismata of increased exercise of faith and love; those of wisdom, knowledge, and discernment of spirits; that of self-restraint; and lastly, that of healing the sick suffering from nervous and psychological diseases. The others for the present are inactive.[21]

Today we live in a unique time. Jean-Jacques Suurmond has observed that, "For the first time the established churches are no longer simply rejecting charismatic spirituality, but are ready to investigate it."[22] It is possible to suggest, with William Dyrness, that God has empowered the Pentecostal movement in recent decades "specifically to remind the church and the role and ministry of the Holy Spirit, especially its role in worship."[23] More specifically, the Pentecostal movement has reminded us that "coming before God is first of all a Spirit-directed event, something that God does in and with his people, by the Spirit." Perhaps this explains why a growing number of Christians have begun to question the traditional cessationist perspective. Take, as one example, the late Presbyterian scholar Donald Bloesch:

> I contend that all of the charisms belong to the wider ministry of the church in every generation. Some have fallen into eclipse, but not because the gifts have ceased with the passing of the apostolic church. Rather, through its desire to control, the

---

21. Kuyper, *The Work of the Holy Spirit*, 188–89.
22. Suurmond, *Word and Spirit at Play*, 74.
23. Dyrness, *A Primer on Christian Worship*, 88–89.

church has grieved and quenched the Spirit so that the Spirit's distribution of the gifts has been impeded . . . The Holy Spirit is conservative in the distribution of his gifts. He grants light only to those who demonstrate by their action that they need light. He gives strength only to those who are exhausting themselves in the struggle to do God's will."[24]

Other scholars, like Suurmond, have advocated for a more prominent role for the Holy Spirit in worship by linking the cessationist perspective to the institutionalization of the church and a corresponding excessive emphasis on church order.[25] He does so with the hope that, perhaps, "the dynamic of the Spirit will finally once again be fully integrated into the church."

The reality of the sovereign Spirit's presence not only fills the gathered community with hope for a dynamic encounter with the Triune God, it also shapes the liturgy or gathering. Thankfully, we don't have to spend time begging the Holy Spirit to join us, nor do we have to expend energy trying to create the right atmosphere within which to feel the Spirit's presence. The Spirit is with us with or without an invitation, whether we feel the Spirit's presence or not. When we pray, then, we need not petition the Spirit's presence, but we best affirm it, as well as the hope which accompanies it. We may also petition for the manifest presence of the Spirit by asking the Spirit's blessing upon our gathering. We do so realizing that without the empowerment of the Spirit, we don't have much hope for anything out of the ordinary. Conversely, with the help of the Spirit, we may expect God to do more than we ask or imagine by His power already at work within us (Eph 3:19).

One prayer that affirms the presence and work of the Holy Spirit among the gathered community is the "Invocation" or opening prayer. In this prayer, we may thank God the Father and, if you are a Western Christian, God the Son for the gift of the Spirit. We may also affirm the presence of the Spirit among us as our hope for dynamic dialogue with our Triune God. Finally, we may confess our sins and acknowledge our limitations before asking the Spirit to work in such a way that the "words of our lips and the meditations of our hearts" may be acceptable to our Triune God.

---

24. Bloesch, *The Holy Spirit*, 294.
25. Suurmond, *Word and Spirit at Play*, 61–74.

Another prayer that affirms the role of the Holy Spirit in worship has traditionally been referred to as the "Prayer for Illumination." Sometimes the content of this prayer is wrapped up in the opening prayer, but, when offered on its own, it usually precedes the Scripture reading and sermon. In this prayer we once again acknowledge our human limitations before seeking the illuminating grace of the Holy Spirit upon the reading and preaching of the Word. Both the Invocation and Prayer for Illumination serve as reminders to the congregation of the unique role of the Spirit.

Finally, with respect to the Holy Spirit, it bears repeating that our hope for a dynamic encounter with the Triune God lies in the Holy Spirit. The gathering of Christians at the invitation of God the Father, in the name of Jesus Christ, with the help of the Holy Spirit is potentially explosive. We gather knowing that our Triune God can do more than we ever ask or imagine. We gather in a space where our Triune God has healed the sick, lifted up the downcast, given a word, and saved the sinner. We gather with expectation believing that the Lord is in the house. We hope to receive afresh the grace and peace of God the Father through our Lord, Jesus Christ, by the power of the Holy Spirit.

This explains why I encourage my students to begin their Sunday services by affirming the presence of God and be articulating hope for a meaningful encounter with Him. I encourage them to remember that those who gather on Sunday have left a world of meaningless "Good Mornings" to spend an hour or more to be in God's presence and to fellowship with God's people. Perhaps, a few have made that choice, not because their lives are filled with hope but, because they long to be greeted with hope. They want to be assured that, in their short time with God's people, they will receive a blessing. And a blessing they will receive. While they may not initially not know it as such, they will experience the grace of our Lord and Savior Jesus Christ, be reminded of the unconditional love of God the Father, and experience authentic fellowship with and through the Holy Spirit.

Conclusion

In short, God the Father calls us to worship, God the Son mediates our worship, and God the Spirit empowers our worship. In this manner, our Triune God shapes how we worship. The question remains whether or not our worship reflects worship of and faith in a Triune God. If someone were to evaluate our Sunday service, reviewing each word and every aspect of the service, would they conclude that our God is three in one? My hunch is that many congregations would answer that question tentatively with "Sometimes," for most congregations struggle finding balance in this area. Most traditions lean more towards one person of the Trinity than another. The old-school Evangelical congregation, for example, clearly focuses on Jesus, while the traditional Pentecostal church highlights the person of the Holy Spirit. As a result, from time to time, a congregation may appear Unitarian or binitarian, instead of Trinitarian. One clear remedy for this tendency is to construct, offer, or even borrow prayers that affirm the Trinity. I close this chapter with one from Eberhard Jüngel.[26]

> Everlasting God, almighty Father, from the beginning you have been our help. You are the source of all good gifts, granting each of us more than we deserve. We give you thanks, and we ask you to open our eyes to the blessings with which you so richly surround us on every side.
>
> Lord Jesus Christ, incarnate God, you have lived our life and suffered our death in order to begin a new life with us. You embrace us in a mystery where we are forever safe. We praise your hidden presence, even as we yearn for the future glory when, fully visible, you will meet us and all the world. Come, Lord Jesus.
>
> God, Holy Spirit, power from on high; you want to burn within us a holy fire. Kindle in us a love for truth that yields an earthly knowledge which does not destroy the secrets of this world but rather enters them protectingly and lovingly. Deem us worthy to know even you, opening our mouths in prayer.

---

26. Jüngel, "Trinitarian Prayers," 246–47.

chapter 3

HOW THE BELOVED SHAPES THE PERSON WHO WORSHIPS

BEST I CAN FIGURE out, with my limited understanding of anthropology, I am a complex but unified and embodied person created in the image of God, born again by the Holy Spirit. That's the person who longs to love the Lord with his worship. That's the person I offer to the Lord as a living sacrifice (Rom 12:1). As such a person, what shall I render to the Lord for all that has been done for me? How shall I worship my Triune God? How shall this complex, unified, embodied person, created in the image of God, and born again by the Holy Spirit, love my Beloved through worship? Here is one attempt to answer those questions. Granted, a moral philosopher may find my reflections rudimentary—and I would agree for they are but one child's attempt to more fully love the Lord through worship.

I Worship as a Complex Albeit Unified Person

When I look in the mirror I see one person, but when I look at my life, I witness complexity. As for the latter, I see a cognitive person who thinks, an emotive person who feels, and a volitional person who makes decisions and acts upon them. Minimally, then, without probing beyond the empirical, I am able to conclude that I am a cognitive, emotive and volitional person. Furthermore, I have observed that when I am healthy and whole, those three *interdependent* systems work harmoniously. My thinking informs my emotions and actions; I need not worry about splitting hairs between my heart and my head.[1] In addition, my emotions and actions generate thoughts that I have not yet articulated; they create "Ah-ha" moments by pointing to values that I have embraced but not yet formally identified.

When I take time to observe other people I find that they, too, are complex but unified persons. I also discover that they differ from me for each person seemingly represents a unique combination of the cognitive, the emotive, and the volitional. Casual observation suggest that with each person, one of those three components either dominates or recedes in significance. Some of my friends are dominated by the cognitive. They are the contemplative types who default to a good book or to one-on-one conversation. Others are more emotive. Like cheerleaders, they are the champagne in the group—always bubbly. Still others can never sit down; they are always doing something. When I add research to my simple observations, I discover that social scientists have engineered tests to quantify the obvious differences between individuals. Consider the perpetual popularity of personality tests and indices, such as the Myers–Briggs, Enneagrams, StrengthsFinder, and others. When all is said and done, I must conclude that each person represents a unique but complex combination of the cognitive, emotive, and the volitional.

Gary Thomas has applied the insights provided by the social sciences to spirituality. In *Sacred Pathways*, he outlines and describes nine personality types or resonant forms of spirituality by which individual Christians grow in their relationship with the Triune God.[2] They are:

1. Naturalists—Loving God Out of Doors
2. Sensates—Loving God With the Senses
3. Traditionalists—Loving God Through Ritual and Symbol
4. Ascetics—Loving God in Solitude and Simplicity
5. Activists—Loving God Through Confrontation
6. Caregivers—Loving God by Loving Others
7. Enthusiasts—Loving God With Mystery and Celebration
8. Contemplatives—Loving God Through Adoration
9. Intellectuals—Loving God With the Mind

---

1. Carey, *Good News for Anxious Christians*, 97–116.
2. Thomas, *Sacred Pathways*.

When I apply the insights of Thomas to my efforts to love my Beloved through worship, I surmise that, in order for me to love the Lord with MY heart, MY soul, MY strength, and MY mind, I will worship my Beloved in a manner consistent with the way I have been wired. Such worship will be wholistic, flowing from the core of my unified personhood. It will be "in my wheel house" or "zone"—an authentic expression of my love for the Lord. Personally, I like a healthy dose of the emotive. I resonate with Jonathan Edwards, who concluded that a cognitive approach to worship often "leaves the individual soul outside as a spectator looking on at the feast."[3] So, I prefer to engage my emotive side in worship. As Edwards asked, "Who can deny that true religion consists in a great measure in vigorous and lively actings of the inclination and will of the soul, or the fervent exercise of the heart?"[4] The Presbyterian Jane Vann agrees by acknowledging that worship "elicits from God's people a broad sweep of emotion."[5] Both echo the conviction of the Psalmist. As N. T. Wright opines, "When the ascended Lord comforts the disturbed and disturbs the comforted, the result is reckless adoration!"[6] Of course, some might find emotion distasteful and disturbing, but that's all right.

> I suspect we all reach a point where somebody else's enthusiasm strikes us as over the top. But, let's face it, the whole point of enthusiasm is that it's over the top; and if you're not enthusiastic about Jesus, or are tempted to mock at somebody who is, look around this story (of Mary anointing the feet of Jesus with oil) and see what company you're keeping.[7]

My unique combination of the emotive, cognitive and volitional, however, may not be held up as a standard for every Christ-follower. As Thomas notes, some Christ-followers, like "Intellectuals who love God with their minds," worship in such a way that the cognitive carries most of the freight. Others, like the "Caregivers" or "Activists" may find worship lacking without a prominent role for the volitional. At the risk of oversimplification, it seems that the worship of the cognitively dominated Christ-follower highlights truth; emotively dominated, celebration; and the volitionally dominated, action. Of course, we are unified, so we can't

---

3. Edwards, *Religious Affections*, 48.
4. Ibid., 24.
5. Vann, *Gathered Before God*, 68-69.
6. Wright, *For All God's Worth*, 88.
7. Ibid.

help but simultaneously engage each aspect of our personhood when we express love for our Beloved through worship.

The recognition that every Christ-follower has been wired differently poses specific challenges for the practice of corporate worship. Authentic worship—that which flows from our complex but unified personhood—looks different for each person. Hence, the gathered community includes individuals with different preferences, a diversity that flows from the unique, internal combination of the cognitive, emotive and volitional. Consequently, when we gather with other Christ-followers, we may expect our brothers and sisters in Christ to worship in a manner different from us. We may not only expect such behavior, but also encourage it, the result of which will be manifold expressions of worship taking place at the same time and place.

What aspect of our complex nature holds the most power to influence and shape our desire to and manner in which we worship our Beloved? Is it our volition? If so, then the key to loving our Beloved through worship is determination, an aspect of our will which can be strengthened through the development of habits (as is the case with addictive behavior). Is it the cognitive? If so, then the key to loving our Beloved through worship is information. Is it the emotive? If so, then the key to loving our Beloved through worship is desire, and the intentional cultivation thereof.

As one who teaches the history of Christianity, in general, and the history of Christian worship, in particular, I think it safe to assume that the Constantinian Church believed that volition is the most persuasive element of human nature. As any monk would have attested, if one cannot discipline the body, there is not much hope for disciplining (and thereby shaping) any other aspect of human nature. Such a conviction explains, in part, the church's emphasis on willful participation in the sacraments during those pre-Reformation days when most saints didn't even understand the language of the liturgy.

During the Reformation, the Protesters replaced the emphasis on the volitional with an emphasis on the cognitive. They believed that the most persuasive element of human nature is the mind. Consequently, they were logocentric. They assumed that if one has correct information, everything else would follow, including proper worship. For that reason much effort was given to transmitting information from one mind to another. That approach worked for me. I was raised within the blessed triangle of a Christian home, Christian church, and Christian day-school.

Ensconced in that environment, my parents, teachers, and pastors introduced me to the person of Jesus Christ. One could say that I began "dating" the Lord at a very young age, gathering information along the way. In time, that information became the foundation of my love for the Lord (emotive) and of my decision to follow him (volition). My experience is not unique. By and large, Protestants have clung to a cognitivist perspective on human nature, one inherited from the Enlightenment. They have defined faith as, first and foremost, the affirmation of and ascent to a body of doctrine concerning the person of Christ. Typically, they emphasize truth about Christ more than a decision to follow Christ.

In recent years, Protestants have come to believe that the emotive is the most persuasive element of human nature, thereby echoing the conviction of classical rhetoric on the generic triad of ethos, pathos, and logos. Perhaps influenced by the advances of the Pentecostal movement and a corresponding appreciation for the person and work of the Holy Spirit, Christ-followers like James K.A. Smith have questioned the adoption of the "Cartesian" definition of personhood wherein our existence is defined by our ability to think. He believes that it has resulted in a "bobble-head Christianity."[8] By contrast, Smith stresses that humans are erotic beings who feel and love, rather than reason, their way through the world.[9] Smith is not alone. Jonathan Haidt, a moral philosopher and social psychologist, argues that people are fundamentally intuitive, not rational.[10] William Saletan, in a review of a book by Haidt, writes, "Drawing on ethnography, evolutionary theory, and experimental psychology, (Haidt) sets out to trash the modern faith in reason."[11] In Saletan's estimation, if you want to persuade others, Haidt insists that you have to recognize the formative power of intuition and appeal to their sentiments for we were "never designed to listen to reason."

Modern Pentecostals and Charismatics don't need scholars like Smith and Haidt to convince them that the emotive is the most persuasive element of human nature. They have been addressing the desires of the heart for over a century. While some have surely crossed the line into irrationality through the exclusive application of the emotive, most have simply acknowledged, either implicitly or explicitly, that a person is

8. Smith, *Desiring the Kingdom*, 39.

9. Ibid., 76.

10. Haidt, *The Righteous Mind*.

11. William Saletan, "Why Won't They Listen," in *New York Times* on March 23, 2012.

more often moved to faith-based action through the emotions which are subsequently affirmed by the cognitive and invigorated by the volitional. I know this is the case for many seeking to break destructive habits. Knowledge of the consequences of a habit upon a person's health doesn't prompt change until that same person realizes that those same consequences hinder or destroy loving relationships with family. My father, for example, finally quit smoking, not because of knowledge gained about the negative impact of smoking on his health, but when the relationships with his wife (my mother) and his five children were nearly terminated due to a stroke and heart attack while forty-something years old. Change was prompted by the emotive element of his complex but unified personhood, a change that allowed him to enjoy fifty years of marriage, witness the development of his children, and enjoy the gift of grandchildren.

As Christ-followers, then, we are complex individuals who think, feel, and act. We think about the Lord. We love the Lord. We serve the Lord. When we are healthy and whole, those three interdependent systems work harmoniously. When we worship, the liturgy will hopefully call each of those systems into action. And if each person worships authentically, that is, in a manner consistent with his or her complex but unified personhood, we will witness the beauty of unity of the faith with diversity of expression.

I Worship as an Embodied Person

WHEN I LOOK IN the mirror I notice that the cognitive, emotive, and volitional aspects of my nature are embodied. Furthermore, life experience has taught me that my body influences the cognitive, emotive, and volitional aspects of my nature. My body, for example, places limits on each aspect of my life. While I may want to dance before the Lord, my body doesn't always allow it. I may desire to read a Psalm in praise to the Lord, but my eyes won't allow it. I may join others and sing praises to the Lord, but not know the language used by others. My body exercises so much influence over the cognitive, emotive, and volitional aspects of my life that little things, like room temperature or allergies, influence my worship.

So I now state the obvious: we worship as embodied saints and our bodies influence the manner in which we worship. Furthermore, we worship with our bodies. On this latter point the Psalmist leave little room for debate:

> "Sing to the Lord!" "Clap your hands to the Lord!" "Kneel before the Lord your maker!" "Rejoice in the Lord!" Humble yourself before the Lord!" "Praise Him with dancing!" "Lift up your hands in the sanctuary!"

The theological foundation for embodied worship is the incarnation of our Savior. Jesus Christ came in the flesh, in a real human body, and that real human body rose from the grave. Few describe the incarnation better than John Updike in his 1960 "Seven Stanzas at Easter."[12]

> Make no mistake: if he rose at all
> It was as His body;
> If the cell's dissolution did not reverse, the molecule reknit,
> The amino acids rekindle,
> The Church will fall.
>
> It was not as the flowers,
> Each soft spring recurrent;
> It was not as His Spirit in the mouths and fuddled eyes of the
> Eleven apostles;
> It was as His flesh; ours.
>
> The same hinged thumbs and toes
> The same valved heart
> That-pierced-died, withered, paused, and then regathered
> Out of enduring Might
> New strength to enclose.
>
> Let us not mock God with metaphor,
> Analogy, sidestepping, transcendence,
> Making of the event a parable, a sign painted in the faded
> Credulity of earlier ages:
> Let us walk through the door.
>
> The stone is rolled back, not papier-mache,
> Not a stone in a story,
> But the vast rock of materiality that in the slow grinding of

---

12. The "Seven Stanzas at Easter" is reprinted from *Telephone Poles and Other Poems* by John Updike. Copyright © 1958, 1959, 1960, 1961, 1962, 1963 by John Updike. Reprinted by permission of Alfred A Knopf, and imprint of Knopf Doubleday Publishing Group, a division of Random House LLC. All rights reserved. Any third-party use of the material, outside of this publication, is prohibited. Interested parties must apply directly to Random House LLC for permission.

> Time will eclipse for each of us
> The wide light of day.
>
> And if we have an angel at the tomb,
> Make it a real angel,
> Weighty with Max Planck's quanta, vivid with hair, opaque in
> The dawn light, robed in real linen
> Spun on a definite loom.
>
> Let us not seek to make it less monstrous,
> For our own convenience, our own sense of beauty,
> Lest, awakened in one unthinkable hour, we are embarrassed
> By the miracle,
> And crushed by remonstrance.

The theological foundation for embodied worship also includes the truth that Jesus Christ came to bring redemption and deliverance to our bodies. Dallas Willard writes.

> The redemption of the body will be completed later, but even now, "if the Spirit of Him who raised Jesus from the dead dwells in you, He who raised Christ Jesus from the dead will also give life to your mortal bodies because of His Spirit who indwells you" (Rom 8:11). We are to know now "the power of the resurrection" (Philippians 3:10). Our body is not just a physical system, but is inhabited by the real presence of Christ.[13]

Since the body is central to our identity as Christ-followers, we may conclude that it must be central to our love of the Beloved. Accordingly, as Willard points out, it makes sense for the person who trusts Christ to present his or her body to the Lord as a living and holy sacrifice, as an act of worship (Rom 12:1–2). "This total yielding of every part of our body to God, until the very tissues and muscles that make it up are inclined toward God and godliness and are vitalized in action by the power of heaven, breaks all conformity with worldly life in this age and transforms us into conformity with the age to come, by completing the renewal of our minds—our powers of thought and imaginations and judgment, deeply rooted in our bodies."[14] On the other hand, writes Willard,

> If the body is simply beyond redemption, then ordinary life is too. Many Christians seem prepared to accept this——at least in practice. But then "spiritual formation" really becomes impossible.

---

13. Willard, *Renovation of the Heart*, 163.
14. Ibid, 170–71.

That would be a defeat of major proportions for Christ's cause, and could never be reconciled with the call to godly living that both permeates the Bible from end to end and resonates with the deep-seated human need to live as one ought.[15]

What are some steps we can take to prepare our bodies for worship? Once again I defer to Dallas Willard. Within a broader conversation on spiritual formation, he offers four suggestions that we can apply specifically to our loving response to God's love. First, through a definitive action let's actually release our body to God. Let's offer our bodies as living sacrifices to the Lord (Romans 12:1). Let us not limit our sacrifice to the mind or the heart. Let us not segment our lives into one event for the body and another event for the mind and another for the heart, or one day for the Lord and six days for ourselves. Let us decide to follow Jesus as embodied persons. The words of Joshua come to mind:

> Now fear the Lord and serve him with all faithfulness. Throw away the gods your ancestors worshiped beyond the Euphrates River and in Egypt, and serve the Lord. But if serving the Lord seems undesirable to you, then choose for yourselves this day whom you will serve, whether the gods your ancestors served beyond the Euphrates, or the gods of the Amorites, in whose land you are living. But as for me and my household, we will serve the Lord (Josh 24:14–15).

Second, let's resist the temptation to idolize the body. Let's not make it an object of ultimate concern. Our bodies belong to God and he can do with them as he pleases. Third, let's not misuse our bodies as either a source of sensual gratification or as a means to dominate or control others. Fourth, let us honor and care for our bodies. Let us regard our bodies as holy or set apart because they are owned and inhabited by God. For that reason, let us nourish, exercise and rest our bodies in preparation for worship.

To that last point, it is tough to separate ourselves from the world, gather with God's people, and love the Lord through worship. It is even more difficult without preparation. As embodied Christ-followers we cannot simply enter a sanctuary, sit down, flick a switch, and worship the Lord with heart, soul, mind, and strength. We are too complex for that to take place. When we gather for worship we bring our sins and experiences, our joys and sorrows, our limited understandings, our tired and broken bodies, our preferences and pains, even our allergies to the

---

15. Willard, "The Human Body and Spiritual Growth."

cologne or perfume on the person next to us. All of that and more make it tough to separate from the world and worship the Lord with his people. As a result, we best prepare for corporate worship with both a good night of sleep and time with the Lord so that when we gather with God's people, we may be fully present in his presence.

I Worship as a Person Created in the Image of God

You and I represent more than embodied persons with cognitive, emotive, and volitional components. As such, we differ little from the animal kingdom. Overarching those elements, we human beings find our strongest motivations, those which ultimately determine everything we do, in our hearts. As you may already foresee, I am not referring to the bodily organ that pumps blood through our veins. Nor am I, in this instance, referring to the emotive component of our humanity. Instead, I am using the word "heart" as it is employed in both the Old and New Testaments: a reference to the whole of the inner being of a person. I understand the heart as the essence or center of a human being. It encompasses the emotive, cognitive, and volitional dimensions of our lives. It includes our conscience (Job 27:6; 1 Sam 25:31) and seems synonymous with soul. It is the place "to which God turns, in which the religious life is rooted, which determines moral conduct."[16] Jonathan Edwards referred to the "heart" as the "religious affections." Others describe it as the seat of our understanding and core of our being. Still others as the image of God. However we understand it, this much is certain: it is the heart that distinguishes human beings from other mammals.

More importantly for this conversation, the heart plays a pivotal role in the worship of the Beloved. Jonathan Edwards noted centuries ago, it is quite possible for me to go through the motions of worship and not worship the Lord with my heart. It is possible for me to talk eloquently about the Lord, offer passionate praise to God, and spend much time practicing worship without my heart. This happens when I am content with a cognitive approach to worship, one that leaves me "outside as a spectator looking on at the feast."[17] It can also happen when we go through the motions and lip-sync our praise, or when we get all emotional about someone or something other than the Lord. Thankfully, during those all-too-frequent

---

16. Kittel and Friedrich, *TDNT*, III:612.
17. Edwards, *Religious Affections*, 48.

occasions when I offer heartless worship, the Holy Spirit keeps working and reminds me that authentic worship involves a "fervent exercise of the heart."[18]

I offer no tips for heart-filled worship except prayer and the aforementioned time of preparation. In particular, I recommend the *Prayer of Examen*. The word *examen*, as Richard Foster notes, "comes from the Latin and refers to the tongue or weight indicator on a balance scale, hence conveying the idea of an accurate assessment of the true situation."[19] Traditionally, a *Prayer of Examen* has "two basic aspects, like two sides of a door." Richard Fosters describes the two aspects in this way: "The first is an *examen of consciousness* through which we discover how God has been present to us throughout the day and how we have responded to his loving presence. The second aspect is an *examen of conscience* in which we uncover those areas that need cleansing, purifying, and healing."[20] While Foster distinguishes two aspects of the *Prayer of Examen*, he also notes that the two, like the waves of the ocean, are "distinct from one another and yet constantly on top of and never totally separate from each other."[21] The benefit of this prayer, according to those have practiced it, is self-knowledge of our sins which, in turn, make us receptive to the Lord who is the only hope to escape our limitations and worship the Lord in *spirit and in truth*. The prayer leaves us at the throne of grace, dependent upon the God the Holy Spirit to inflame our hearts with love for our Beloved.

I Worship as a Temple of the Holy Spirit

Up to this point, my reflections could be applied to any person—Christian or not. That which distinguishes our worship as Christ-followers from the worship of others, such as the Muslims and Buddhists, is not limited to the doxological norms of the Bible. It includes the indwelling presence of the Holy Spirit. Through the presence and power of the Holy Spirit, we may worship our Beloved in a manner which reflects the presence and power of the Holy Spirit. The magnitude of that worship lies beyond our comprehension, for the Holy Spirit, as the third person

18. Ibid., 24.
19. Foster, *Prayer*, 27.
20. Ibid., 27–28.
21. Ibid., 32.

of the Trinity, can do in and through us more than we can ask or imagine. However, the apostle Paul helps us understand how the Holy Spirit typically works in our worship, beginning with the spiritual gifts of faith, hope, and love—three gifts of the Holy Spirit, three theological virtues, three essentials for the one who desires to love the Lord through worship. Without faith, I have no High Priest to take my broken prayers to the throne of heaven (Heb 4:14–16). Without hope, I have no expectation of dialogue with the Lord whose love prompts my worship. Without love, my worship clangs like a cymbal played out of place (I Cor 13:1).

It takes faith, hope, and love to worship the Lord, but that is easier said than done. We come to the Lord with doubt-filled faith, guarded hope, and limited love. Yet, as a temple of the Holy Spirit, each believer may worship the Lord, cognizant of those deficiencies and confident that the Holy Spirit will compensate for his or her weaknesses. The apostle John assures us that the power of the Spirit within us is greater than our deficiencies (1 John 4:4). The apostle Paul offers similar words of encouragement by assuring us that we can do all things by the power already at work within us (Phil 4:13). In addition, the Lord speaks to us the very words he spoke to Paul: "My grace is sufficient for you, for my power is made perfect in weakness" (2 Cor 12:9).

It takes faith, hope, and love to worship the Lord, "but the greatest of these is love" (1 Cor 13:13). Worship, at its core, is our loving response to our Beloved. In I Corinthians 13, we discover the apostle Paul's remarkable teaching on love. In it, he affirms the indisputable relationship between love and worship. As noted in my "Introduction," Paul teaches us that without love, our ritual acts of worship, even the spectacular, don't amount to much in the eyes of our Triune God. He contests our tendency to accept—even prioritize—the external without regard to the internal, liturgical practices without regard to the motivation. He encourages us to hope and pray that our acts of worship will always flow from the fountain of grateful, humble, loving hearts.

Paul also asserts that love "is a more excellent blessing than any of the extraordinary ecstatic gifts of the Spirit."[22] More specifically, Paul teaches that the gift of love trumps the gifts of prophecy, tongues, miracles, and preaching. Surely, God blessed Moses as a leader, David as a poet and king, Elijah as a prophet, Daniel as an interpreter of dreams, the apostles as miracle-workers, and Paul as an evangelist. Yet for Paul,

---

22. Edwards, *Charity and Its Fruits*, 30.

the gift of love is greater than each of those gifts. We may conclude that the Christian, in whom the Holy Spirit works the grace of love, is more greatly blessed than any prophet, king, or apostle. This may explain the passionate exhortation of Jonathan Edwards:

> Earnestly seek this blessed fruit of the Spirit, and let us seek that it may abound in our souls; that the love of God may more and more be shed abroad in our hearts; and that we may love the Lord Jesus Christ in sincerity, and love one another as Christ hath loved us. (Then) we shall possess the richest of all treasures, and the highest and most excellent of all graces.[23]

Thanks be to God that each believer is and worships as a temple of the Holy Spirit. The very same Spirit that raised Jesus from death is with us. The very same Spirit that showered the church in Jerusalem that first Pentecost is with us. The very same Spirit who gifts us with faith, hope and love is with us each time we gather for worship. And for these reasons, we gather each week with expectation that though weak, we will be strong in faith, hope, and love.

I Worship Virtuously

Protestant Christians don't talk much about virtue but those who came before us did. The pre-Reformation theological tradition includes a distinction between two types of virtues: the theological and the cardinal. The three theological virtues—those by which we receive God's grace—are faith, hope and love. The cardinal virtues—those produced in our lives with the help of the Holy Spirit—include prudence, courage, temperance, and justice. In more recent years, our understanding of virtues has been expanded. The list of virtues now includes moral excellences or positive character traits of people, such as kindness, honesty, and humility. In modern conversation about virtues, it is understood that such qualities require cultivation, development, and practice. As Peter Kreeft notes, sanctification requires the Spirit as well as our rigorous cooperation, contra much of the Protestant world:

> But isn't it true that righteousness, a righteousness far surpassing the four cardinal virtues, becomes available to us when we are joined to Christ? It certainly is. And isn't this a supernatural righteousness, a fruit of the Holy Spirit himself? Absolutely. But

---

23. Ibid., 321–22.

supernatural virtue is not subnatural virtue. It does not dispense with natural human foundation and with our responsibility to be active, not passive, in cultivation of virtuous habits.[24]

It is also understood that such qualities enrich our lives with fulfillment, peace, and happiness. As the author of Hebrews reminds us, even unpleasant discipline yields a harvest of righteousness and peace (Heb 12:11).

Why all this talk about virtue? Because the Scriptures prescribe that the worship of individual Christians be characterized by specific virtues. I highlight two: humility and joy. Humility is especially important for the individual Christ-follower who gathers with other Christ-followers for corporate worship (1 Pet 5:5–6). When I gather for corporate worship with my brothers and sisters in Christ, I must humble myself, not only before God, but before the liturgy. I must agree to participate in the service that has been formed by those delegated with this responsibility. By so doing, I prioritize corporate worship over personal preferences and make corporate worship possible for me. The decision to humble myself before the liturgy has consequences besides the obvious: freeing me from the sin of approaching corporate worship as a consumer. First, it strengthens my rapport with fellow believers. When I subordinate my tastes for the sake of others, spiritual unity increases. Furthermore, as a corollary to this, as I practice the discipline of submission, my Christian character is deepened.

Joy is another virtue that characterizes my worship. The testimony of Scripture is clear on this point. Here are a few examples:

- "Rejoice in the Lord and be glad" (Ps 32:11).
- "Take delight in the Lord" (Ps 37:4).
- "Sing to God, sing in praise of his name, extol him who rides on the clouds; rejoice before him—his name is the Lord" (Ps 68:4).

Those admonitions accompany the testimony of the Psalmist, who sang, "You turned my wailing into dancing; you removed my sackcloth and clothed me with joy, that my heart may sing your praises and not be silent" (Ps 30:11–12). They also offer an explanation for King David's exuberant display of joy while leading the Ark of the Covenant back to its home in Jerusalem (2 Sam 6). Perhaps John Piper had David in mind when he

---

24. Kreeft, *Back to Virtue*, 67.

wrote, "We feel an unencumbered joy in the manifold presence of God—the joy of gratitude, wonder, hope, admiration.... We are satisfied with the excellency of God and we overflow with the joy of his fellowship."[25]

The relationship between worship and joy brings us to an apparent contradiction. It is not uncommon to hear a well-meaning Christ-follower say something like "worship is not about us; it's about God." That statement sounds so true that it usually generates a spontaneous "Amen" or "Hallelujah" or "Praise the Lord." But is it true? Surely, when it comes to the content of worship, it *is* all about God. With the words of our lips and meditations of our hearts we lift up the grandeur and glory of our Triune God. We may even sing the first verse of the Stuart Keene Hine (1899–1989) hymn, "How Great Thou Art":

> O Lord my God, When I in awesome wonder,
> Consider all the worlds Thy Hands have made;
> I see the stars, I hear the rolling thunder,
> Thy power throughout the universe displayed.
>
> Then sings my soul, My Saviour God, to Thee,
> How great Thou art, How great Thou art.
> Then sings my soul, My Saviour God, to Thee,
> How great Thou art, How great Thou art!

But we will not stop there for worship is our loving response to what God has done for us. So we will also sing:

> And when I think, that God, His Son not sparing;
> Sent Him to die, I scarce can take it in;
> That on the Cross, my burden gladly bearing,
> He bled and died to take away my sin.
>
> Then sings my soul, My Saviour God, to Thee,
> How great Thou art, How great Thou art.
> Then sings my soul, My Saviour God, to Thee,
> How great Thou art, How great Thou art!

In a manner of speaking, then, worship is not just about God. As my friend and colleague Michael Quicke writes, "worship is a 360-degree experience."[26] We find ourselves in the middle of a circle that both begins and ends with our Triune God who begins the process by creating us in his image and loving us. It is worth noting here that part of the image of

---

25. Piper, *Desiring God*, 85.
26. Quicke, *Preaching as Worship*, 83–101.

God within us is the reflection of the overflowing joy which is intrinsic to our Triune God. Willard writes:

> We pay a lot of money to get a tank with a few tropical fish in it and never tire of looking at their brilliant iridescence and marvelous forms and movements. But God has *seas full of them*, which he constantly enjoys . . . (God) is simply one great inexhaustible and eternal experience of all that is good and true and beautiful and right. This is what we must think of when we hear theologians and philosophers speak of him as a perfect being. *This is his life*.[27]

This Triune God has loved us beyond measure and this love has the power to inflame hearts in such a way that we long to respond to God's love with love. As Frederick M. Lehman once wrote,

> O love of God, how rich and pure!
> How measureless and strong!
> It shall forevermore endure
> The saints' and angels' song.[28]

Overwhelmed by God's love words like these flow freely from the lips of the beloved of God: "I love the Lord, for he heard my voice; he heard my cry for mercy. Because he turned his ear to me, I will call on him as long as I live" (Ps 116:1–2). Hence, after receiving his love, we offer loving worship to God, our Beloved. Since worship constitutes our loving response to God's amazing grace, why wouldn't we? This means that while the content of our worship is all about God and the motivation for worship is what God has done for us, the praxis of worship depends on our willingness to realize and embody our affections for the Trine God.

Here, then, is the irony: worship is not just about our Triune God; it is also about us. We play an essential role in the worship experience. We are the beloved of God who have chosen to respond to God's love by loving the Lord, our beloved, through worship. We are the blessed of God, the wife of Yahweh, who bursts into song and shouts for joy (Isa 54:1–6). As Piper notes, "the person who has the vague notion that it is virtue to overcome self-interest, and that it is vice to seek pleasure, will scarcely be able to worship."[29] The spirit of worship is killed by the insistence that every act of worship be free from self-interest.

---

27. Willard, *Divine Conspiracy*, 63.
28. Chorus of the hymn *The Love of God*, written by Frederick M. Lehman in 1919.
29. Piper, *Desiring God*, 87.

But there's more going on here. As noted above, God has created us in his image to worship him. As a result, we long, even need to worship. When we worship, then, we experience the kind of joy that rises from harmony within our parts. There is a sense that when we worship we are the people God created us to be. Add to that this observation by Augustine: God has created us with a desire to be happy and in such a way that what governs our will is that with which we delight. So, with one hand, God has created us to worship him. With the other, God has created us with a desire to be happy. As a result, we experience happiness when we worship the Lord. When we worship God, we experience joy. From this we should not conclude that we are motivated to worship by selfish desires. Instead, we are motivated by a God-ordained desire to be happy. At times we may choose where and how to find happiness, but we can never change the ultimate source of happiness. We will remain unhappy until we find our delight in the Lord.

Conclusion

"What shall I return to the Lord for all his goodness to me? (Ps 116:12). How shall I—a complex but unified and embodied person, created in the image of God and born again by the Holy Spirit—worship my loving God? The Psalmist answers his own question with, "I will lift up the cup of salvation and call on the name of the Lord. I will fulfill my vows to the Lord in the presence of all his people" (13–14). With those words, the Psalmist touches on the relationship between the love of God and the shape of our worship. The pattern seems clear: God loves us and in response we love God but long to do so with an eye on what pleases God. Worship, then, is first and foremost our loving response to our Triune God's amazing love for us. The impulse of love, furthermore, encourages us to allow our worship to be shaped by our Beloved, the one who best determines the shape of the lover's love.

I wish I could write that I have arrived there and that I love the Lord with all my heart, soul, mind, and strength. I haven't. Something within me, typically referred to as selfishness, prohibits me from giving my all to the Lord. I love with most of myself, but not all. Truth be told, if a scientist dissected me into parts, she would discover that I love with a fraction of myself. I hope my love for the Lord is better today than it was yesterday and that it will be better tomorrow than it is today. This much I know: it will always be a work in progress.

Nevertheless, I have discovered that my imperfect love for the Lord helps me clarify the challenges of loving the Lord, even while I worship, with all my heart, soul, mind, and strength. First, I struggle respecting those who worship differently from me. Sure, I can handle it once or twice a year, during annual ecumenical services or the like. On those occasions I welcome diverse expressions of worship. I find them interesting, if not entertaining. But when I gather with my covenanted community of believers, I silently expect uniformity of expression. Of course, as I shall note in greater detail in the next section, a certain amount of uniformity is required for corporate worship. Those gathered in a particular place at a particular time must humble themselves before a common liturgy so that they may worship the Lord as one body with one voice. But how much uniformity shall we expect? How much diversity shall we expect? How do uniformity and diversity in worship reflect our unity or lack of unity in Christ?

Second, I question whether, in some contexts, it is best that I worship sincerely but not authentically. Occasionally I gather with Christians whose "heart language" differs significantly from my own. In other words, I worship with a congregation that reads every part of the liturgy, except for the sermon and the Lord's Supper. Personally, I struggle with liturgiesfilled with unison and responsive readings; I just don't connect with them. I wonder, then, is it OK to fake it? And to do so sincerely? Shall I pocket my hands instead of raising them to the Lord when I find myself with a community of Christians who worship the Lord without their hands? Shall I read the responsive or unison reading even though I don't want to? Shall I sit when I get tired of standing or wait for everyone else to sit? Shall I stand when the excellences of God's grace starti pushing me to my feet or shall I wait till someone tells me to stand? Shall I sing the song even though I just don't like it? Where is the joy when my participation in the liturgy flows from God's mandate to humble myself for the sake of others? Shall my joy come from witnessing the joy of others or from my simple act of obedience? Or shall it come from the knowledge that Christ mediates my half-baked worship?

Third, I struggle designing corporate worship services which encourage authentic worship by all those gathered. I hope to design liturgies that address the cognitive, emotive, and volitional components of the human being. I hope to design liturgies that allow for growth in the knowledge of the Lord, cultivation of love for the Lord, and acts of service to the Lord. Typically, however, my liturgies lean toward one of the three components of human personhood. But what happens if they lean so heavy to one mode that many in the congregation don't find opportunity to worship authentically? What if the cognitively dominantly folk don't get enough meat to chew on? Or the emotively dominantly folk go through the liturgy and don't feel like they worshiped? Or the volitionally dominantly folk don't receive enough opportunities to serve? Although the challenge of engaging each of our human dimensions in the context of gathered worship can be frustrating, it is also dynamic and fruitful: it forces us to examine critically both ourselves and the "love language" of our heavenly Bridegroom.

chapter 4

HOW THE BELOVED SHAPES THE PEOPLE WHO WORSHIP

MUCH HAS BEEN WRITTEN in recent years about the mission of our Triune God, especially among those in the "missional movement."[1] From this impressive pile of literature we find agreement on this much: *The mission of our Triune God is not just to save individuals but to create a people.* There may be disagreement on the particulars of how this people lives together and bears witness to Christ in their neighborhoods, but Christ-followers agree that the core of God's mission is the creation of a people.[2] As Walter Burghardt once said, "Our incredibly imaginative Triune God had in mind not billions of isolated humans scattered around a globe, basically independent each of every other. God has in mind a people, a human family, a community of persons, a body genuinely one."[3]

We discover that mission in the book of Genesis when the Lord makes this promise to Abraham: "I will make you into a great nation and I will bless you" (Gen 12:1). Centuries later the apostle Peter, the rock of the Church, affirmed God's mission with these words to Christ-followers: "You are a chosen people, a royal priesthood, a holy nation, God's special possession, that you may declare the praises of him who called you out of darkness into his wonderful light. Once you were not a people, but now

---

1. See, as an example, Fitch, *The Great Giveaway.*

2. See Watts, "The New Exodus/New Creational Restoration in the Image of God," 15–41.

3. Burghardt, *Christ in Ten Thousand Places.*

you are the people of God; once you had not received mercy, but now you have received mercy" (1 Pet 2:9–10). The Apocalypse of John also affirms that the mission of God is to create a people (Rev 21).[4] John's detailed description of the holy city may distract us from recognizing that the New Jerusalem is not a place but a people. It is not the final home of the redeemed, it is the redeemed! It is the church, a real and precious community that enjoys eternal fellowship with God in a new heaven and new earth.[5] We may conclude then, that when we gather, we represent more than the aggregate sum of our beings. We are a holy nation, a people set apart by God. We are a royal priesthood, that is, a people called by God to offer sacrifices of praise. And we, a bunch of ragamuffins, are a people who belong to God. Furthermore, our value as a people of God derives, not from the nobility of certain outstanding individuals, but rather from the fact that the whole corporate body is adopted by God (1 Cor 1:26–31).

Such an understanding of the local church harmonizes with our understanding of the one, holy, catholic, and apostolic Church. As the Heidelberg Catechism notes, "Jesus, through his Spirit and Word, out of the entire human race, from the beginning of the world to its end, gathers, protects, and preserves for himself, a community chosen for eternal life and united in true faith."[6] This community is a not an abstract theory, but a real people of God in the world, a real spiritual society, a real body of Christ actually present in the world, a place where the light of God really shines and the life of God really pulses.[7] Furthermore, it is a community called together by the Lord.

Returning to the theme of the mission of God, let's note that it hasn't changed much over the years, if at all. Until the return of Christ, the Lord

---

4. See Hamstra, "An Idealist View of Revelation," 93–131.

5. John's vision of "mission accomplished" includes several notable elements. The holy city does not require natural or artificial light since the glory of God gives it light and the Lamb is its lamp (Rev 21:11,23; 22:5). The city is without a sanctuary for the Lord God and the Lamb are its temple (21:22). As a result, believers as a royal priesthood have direct and immediate fellowship with God (Jer 31:33; John 4:23,24; Heb. 8:8). The throne of God is within the city; from this location our Lord reigns with love (Rev 22:3–4). Finally, the size of the city is too large for imagination because it includes citizens from every nation (21:24). Taken together, these elements show that the mission of God includes the merging of heaven and earth. Creation, then, is not destroyed but rather "the unification of heaven and earth is such that the renewed earth itself becomes Yahweh's throne room." For this last point, see Watts, "The New Exodus/New Creational Restoration of the Image of God," 36.

6. The Heidelberg Catechism Lord's Day 21, Answer 54.

7. Newbigin, *The Household of God*, 53.

continues to shape a people who belong to him, a people with whom to enjoy fellowship, now and throughout eternity. Our mission as a congregation, then, is simple: *to live out our identity as a people who belong to God*. Much like a nuclear family, our mission is to be the people God has called us to be.

As we fulfill our mission we embrace the threefold orientation of Jesus (Matt 14:23) who pulled away from people, went to the wilderness, and looked up to his father in heaven. He then looked in and fellowshipped with small groups of disciples. Finally, he looked out upon and entered a broken world with compassion and grace. Like our Savior, we seek to embrace a threefold orientation, both as individual believers and as the church. We dedicate ourselves to looking upward, inward, and outward. We look up to our Triune God, look in to our community of Christ-followers, and look out to our world.[8]

Our mission as a people of God has remained relatively unchanged since the creation of Adam and Eve, and so has our purpose. In what may be the only purpose statement for the church in the New Testament, the apostle Peter writes: "You are a chosen people . . . so that you may declare the praises of him who called you out of darkness into his wonderful light (1 Pet 2:9). The Westminster Shorter Catechism of 1640 echoes those words by affirming that our purpose is "to glorify God and enjoy him forever."

When we combine our mission, purpose, and threefold orientation into one cluster, we receive a vision of our future as local congregations. In summary, we live out our identify as the people of God by looking up and declaring the glory of God in worship, looking in and declaring the glory of God to one another, and looking out and declaring the glory of God to our world. More specifically, we fulfill our destiny as the people of God when we worship our Triune God, enjoy fellowship with our brothers and sisters in Christ, and touch a portion of the world with the mercy, justice, and grace of our Lord.

The People of God

The comprehension and affirmation of our identity as a people of God holds great potential to shape our lives, especially our corporate response to his love. First, it encourages us to insist that our corporate gatherings

---

8. Breen and Cochran, *Developing a Discipleship Culture*.

reflect our identity as a unified people, not just a collective of individuals. We are a family, a fellowship, a community, a communion of saints. As such, we must resist the temptation to view our weekly gathering as merely a collection of individuals who gather to simultaneously engage in a predetermined list of actions and practices. We are more than a group of individuals who happen to be in the same place at the same time. We represent more than a crowd at a game, a group at a political rally, or a collective of people enjoying a meal at a restaurant. Even though we gather as individual Christ-followers, we participate in something far greater than the sum of our parts. We are the chosen people of God.

Even with our identity firmly settled, occasionally we approach the weekly gathering of God's people as a private affair. We are not alone. The air we breathe in North American society and North American Protestantism encourages individualism. Consequently, more often than we care to admit, we gather with other Christ-followers as individual consumers seeking spiritual nourishment or as spectators who happen to be sitting in the same place at the same time for the same purpose. We know we have fallen to the temptation of individualism when, while gathering with others for worship, we give little attention to our neighbor. I am sure I am not the only Christ-follower who has isolated him or herself from others while gathering for corporate worship. If truth be told, it is not unusual for us to offer a few verbal pleasantries to people we see on the way (or in our way) while walking from our car in the parking lot to the gathering space. After taking our place in the sanctuary, we offer personal prayers and praise to God, leave the presence of the gathered community, hop in our cars, and return to our lives. It is as though we gathered in the same room with Christ but did not take time to fellowship with him. Thankfully God forgives us and reaffirms our identity as his people. He invites us, over and over again, to gather as a people for worship in the name of Jesus and by power of the Holy Spirit.

But now let's move to the main question of this chapter: How does our identity as a people of God shape the worship of our Beloved? First, it surely shapes how we gather. Let's take our cue from others who gather as a people with a shared identity. Perhaps you remember the last time you gathered with your uncles and aunts, your cousins and grandparents. Perhaps you gathered to celebrate the marriage of a niece. If you gathered like my family gathers, you greeted your family members. You talked, shook hands, hugged, and kissed. (If of Greek extraction, you kissed or air-kissed both cheeks of each person you hugged.) For those you hadn't seen in a while, you saved more demonstrative greetings. For those you didn't know, such as your niece's fiancé's family, you offered a personal introduction.

When we gather as the people of God, we reflect some of the same. I understand that such a vision does not resonate with that of congregations which gather quietly and reservedly. In such contexts, individuals often arrive with little fanfare before sitting silently in the sanctuary where they prepare their hearts for worship. That ritual may have some merit. I am reminded of Dietrich Bonhoeffer's admonition to his seminarians that they remain silent while gathering for morning prayers. As in monastic practices, he desired that the first words heard each day would be the Word of God.[9] But should not that method of gathering be the exception, rather than the norm? Should we not prepare ourselves for corporate worship before gathering with our community of believers, then greet those with whom we worship? Why isolate ourselves from those with whom we are gathering for worship? Is not such a practice akin to attending a family party and sitting alone in an empty room? Should not the means by which we gather affirm and celebrate our identity as a family of God?

Our identity as a people of God, however, does more than shape how we gather for worship; it shapes how we worship our Beloved. The Bible highlights several characteristics of the people of God which significantly shape the worship of our Beloved. I begin with love.

A Loving People

While tempted to do so, we cannot separate loving worship of our Beloved from love to one another. The vertical and horizontal dimensions to the Greatest Commandment (Mark 12:30) give shape to a 360 degree worship experience.[10] We who have been loved by God, desire to love God in return. But we can't love God in worship without loving those with whom we worship. As James wrote,

> With the tongue we praise our Lord and Father, and with it we curse human beings, who have been made in God's likeness. Out of the same mouth come praise and cursing. My brothers and sisters, this should not be. Can both fresh water and salt

---

9. See Bonhoeffer, *Life Together*, 43.
10. See Quicke, *Preaching as Worship*.

> water flow from the same spring? My brothers and sisters, can a fig tree bear olives, or a grapevine bear figs? Neither can a salt spring produce fresh water (Jas 3:9–12).

So, following the teaching of the apostle Paul, we seek to love all people, "especially those who belong to the family of believers" (Gal 6:10).

The biblical foundation for this 360 degree experience may be drawn from the letters of the apostle John, the apostle Paul, and the words of Jesus who invites us to lives of love. In his first epistle to the Corinthians, Paul affirms the essential place of love in worship by nullifying all acts of worship which are not motivated by love for God. John expands that teaching by requiring love for both our Beloved and the beloved of God (those with whom we worship). He ties a tight knot between them in his first epistle:

> Dear friends, let us love one another, for love comes from God. Everyone who loves has been born of God and knows God. Whoever does not love does not know God, because God is love. This is how God showed his love among us: He sent his one and only Son into the world that we might live through him. This is love: not that we loved God, but that he loved us and sent his Son as an atoning sacrifice for our sins. Dear friends, since God so loved us, we also ought to love one another. No one has ever seen God; but if we love one another, God lives in us and his love is made complete in us (1 John 4:7–12).

John revisits this theme in his second epistle. There we find these words to the bride of Christ:

> And now, dear lady, I am not writing you a new command but one we have had from the beginning. I ask that we love one another. And this is love: that we walk in obedience to his commands. As you have heard from the beginning, his command is that you walk in love. (2 John 5–6)

Augustine aptly summarizes the apostle John's teaching with these comments: "When therefore you love the members of Christ, you love Christ; when you love Christ, you love the Son of God; when you love the Son of God, you also love the Father. Love therefore cannot be separated into parts. Choose what you love; all the rest will follow."[11] Or, as the

---

11. Aumann, *Christian Spirituality*, 18.

Methodist bishop Rueben Job wrote, "Do no harm, do good, and stay in love with God."[12]

The apostle John challenges our tendency to limit love to those who love us, but it also encourages us with the good news that the power to love is found in God. In fact, those born of God will find within their inner being an eternal fountain of love from which to draw while loving others (John 7:38). The apostle Paul assures us of much the same by including love in our sevenfold unity as Christians (Eph 4:4–7). While we will explore this gift of grace in the next section, suffice to say at this point that Paul views love or *agape* as an essential ingredient of our life together as Christians.

Clearly, both John and Paul simply remix the teaching of Jesus who, in Matthew 22:37–39, summarized the essence of the Christian life by bringing together injunctions from Deuteronomy 6 and Lev 19: neighbor-love and God-love in the Torah as love for God and neighbor. Then, at the Last Supper, as Jordon Aumann notes, "Christ gives love an entirely new dimension, not only by relating love of neighbor to the love of God, but by placing love of neighbor in a central position in the Christian life."[13]

> A new command I give you: Love one another. As I have loved you, so you must love one another. By this everyone will know that you are my disciples, if you love one another . . . As the Father has loved me, so have I loved you. Now remain in my love. If you keep my commands, you will remain in my love, just as I have kept my Father's commands and remain in his love. I have told you this so that my joy may be in you and that your joy may be complete. My command is this: Love each other as I have loved you (John 13:34–35; 15:9–12).

Our loving fellowship as local congregations is both a gift of grace and a command. When we draw from the well of God's love and love one another, we experience a love far deeper and richer than the fellowship we may have as family or friends. This divine love supersedes the fellowship we may have had as immigrants speaking a common language. It flows from the Holy Spirit of God by whose power we may respond to the love of God with both love for our Beloved and for others. And our love for others, like the love of God, will break down barriers and overcome

---

12. Job, *Three Simple Rules*.
13. Aumann, *Christian Spirituality*, 16.

prejudices; it will be beyond our comprehension (Ephesians 2:19–20), but not our aspirations.

We witness the fruit of such dynamism among those in the first church of Jerusalem. Gilbert Bilizekian summarizes that unique and amazing event in this way.

> There was once a community of believers ... so totally devoted to God that their life together was charged with the Spirit's power. In that band of Christ-followers, believers loved each other with a radical kind of love. They took off their masks and shared their lives together. They laughed and cried and prayed and sang and served together in authentic Christian fellowship. Those who had more shared freely with those who had less until socioeconomic barriers melted away. People related together in ways that bridged gender and racial chasms, and celebrated cultural differences. Acts 2 tells us that this community of believers, this church, offered unbelievers a vision of life that was so beautiful it took their breath away. It was so bold, so creative, so dynamic that they couldn't resist it.[14]

"People who belong to such a community," writes Rodney Clapp, "want to belong to it. They cannot imagine worthwhile life without it."[15]

But that may not be your experience of church. As early as the Garden of Eden, the gift of community has been disrupted. Satan entered a perfect garden and subverted the fellowship of the first couple, Adam and Eve. Years later, Satan entered the heart of Cain who murdered Abel and subverted the fellowship of the first family. Still later, Satan entered the hearts of people who constructed a tower of Babel, not for the sake of community, but for themselves. Since that time, Satan has entered countless congregations and subverted their fellowship in Christ. While all that is tragic, even more so is the widespread neglect of the gift of community among congregations. Too few Christians even recognize threats to community, confess their failures in maintaining community, and don't experience a loving community. In modern conversations, we have even found it possible to use the phrase "worship wars" without recognizing that there can be no worship of our Beloved when the beloved of God are at war. The cold, hard, biblical facts, then, are that many congregations on many occasions fail to worship the Lord in a manner pleasing to him.

---

14. In Hybels, *Courageous Leadership*, 17–18.
15. Clapp, *A Peculiar People*, 187–211.

As a result, their corporate worship is but a "resounding gong or clanging symbol" (1 Cor 13:1) to the ears of our Triune God.

There is an alternative. The apostle Paul offers plenty of direction for congregations seeking to respond to God's love with both love for the Beloved and for the people of God. In a series of mandates, each of which includes the phrase "One another," he tells us how we should live as people who love both our Triune God and one another:

- Romans 12:10—Honor one another above yourselves.
- Romans 12:16—Live in harmony with one another.
- Romans 14:12—Don't pass judgment on one another.
- Romans 15:7—Accept one another as Christ has accepted you.
- Romans 15:14—Instruct one another.
- Romans 16:16—Greet one another with a holy kiss.
- I Corinthians 1:10—Agree with one another.
- Galatians 5:13—Serve one another in love!
- Ephesians 4:2—Bear with one another in love.
- Ephesians 4:32—Be kind and compassionate to one another.
- Ephesians 5:19—Speak to one another with psalms, hymns, spiritual songs.
- Ephesians 5:21—Submit to one another!
- Colossians 3:16—Admonish one another!
- I Thessalonians 5:11—Encourage one another.

Surely we hope that every Christian congregation or church family covenants to love one another in the manner prescribed by Paul. Surely we pray that every Christian community of believers will seek to be so united in love that the world takes notice and glorifies God (John 17:21). Surely we strive "to distinguish ourselves as authentic Christian communities" which offer loving worship to our Triune God while, as Paul prescribes, rejoicing in diversity, getting to know one another intimately, and making certain that each person plays an essential role.[16] Surely we diligently pursue "wholistic environments (within which) people of all capacities and fallibilities are incorporated, creativity is multiplied rather

---

16 Balswick and Balswick, *The Family*, 359–60.

than channeled, (and) individualized responses are characteristic."[17] Surely these are our prayers, our aspirations, and our hopes.

But what are the practical implications of being a people called to corporate worship characterized by love for our Beloved and love for our brothers and sisters in Christ? How does that call shape our liturgy? While those questions must be answered by particular congregations in specific places at certain times, I suggest congregations explore these two areas: multigenerational worship and communal rituals. Multigenerational worship provides a covenanted community with the opportunity for up to four generations of Christ-followers to worship as one. Multigenerational worship also includes a unique set of questions for those planning weekly liturgies. How will the liturgy allow multiple generations to worship together? How does our love for one another shape our answer to that question? How does the love of grandparents and grandchildren for one another shape the liturgy of those same people? In other words, *what's love got to do with it*? Communal or ecclesiastical rituals also provide opportunities for congregations to express love for God and one another. Rituals such as congregational prayers, personal testimonies, and even announcements about life together open up avenues for the sharing of life and love. Through such actions we express and build our community as brothers and sisters in Christ. In the announcements, for example, we share housekeeping matters peculiar to our church life, such as the time, place, and date for a particular gathering or ministry; we verbally highlight joys and concerns so that we may "rejoice with those who rejoice and mourn with those who mourn" (Rom 12:15); we acknowledge, even applaud momentous events in the lives of individual members, such as the birth of a child or a 50th anniversary of a marriage or an engagement to be married. We also update our prayer lists with the names of those who have lost health or love or life. So while announcements are not an act of worship, they hold an important place in the liturgy as a means of expressing our love for one another—a love without which we can't truly worship our Beloved.

One People

While Jesus was on earth, he offered this prayer to his Father in heaven: "I pray for those who will believe in me through their message, that

---

17. McKnight, *The Careless Society*, 167.

all of them may be one" (John 17:20–21). While sectarianism and denominationalism may lead us to conclude otherwise, God the Father has answered the prayer of his son. The apostle says as much with these words: we are "one body, united by one Spirit, called to one hope, in one Lord, to one faith and one baptism in Jesus Christ, and have been created and called by one God who is over all and through all and in all" (Eph 4:4–6). This means that while a congregation includes an eclectic group of individuals from two-year-olds to eighty-two-year-olds, it is one body. When we gather for worship, we leave behind our differences and barriers to become one body, and thereby, reflect the God-given gift of our sevenfold unity.

The affirmation of our unity as a gathered community impacts the words we use to greet one another. When I gather with my church community, for example, I leave behind the titles of the workplace or the world. Instead of being referred to as "Doctor," a title granted to me in academic settings, I am called by my first name or by my function (pastor). The same could be said of any person whose status in the public sphere is accompanied by an honorific title. On Monday, you may be greeted with "Captain" or "Your Honor" or "Mayor," but on Sunday you will be greeted as a member of the family where we often make distinctions based on function, but not on status.

Our sevenfold unity as a congregation is first a gift of grace, then an obligation. As the apostle Paul wrote, "Make every effort to keep the unity of the Spirit through the bond of peace" (Eph 4:3). Echoing Paul, the twentieth-century Confession of Belhar states the following: "Through the working of God's Spirit (our unity) is a binding force, yet simultaneously a reality which must be earnestly pursued and sought: one which the people of God must continually be built up to attain."[18]

We need the Belhar Confession and other such reminders because of the divisive power of sin. Unity, like salvation, is an ontological fact, but one which requires effort to manifest in our experience. Left to our own devices—the pride of life, the lust of the flesh, and the lust of the eyes—there is little hope for unity. The realization of our limitations, even sinfulness, brings us to the throne of grace seeking both forgiveness and a new heart. With those gifts in place, we put ourselves, once again, to the task of reflecting our God-given sevenfold unity. Such efforts will inevitably lead us to the "Sermon on the Mount," where Jesus describes

18. *Confession of Belhar*, Article 2.

the link between our relation with others and the worship of our Beloved. In fact, Jesus encourages us to repair fractured relationships with fellow Christians before we worship with them: "If you are offering your gift at the altar and there remember that your brother has something against you, leave your gift there in front of the altar. First go and be reconciled to your brother; then offer your gift" (Matt 5:23–24).

Traditionally, some Christians have linked Jesus' teaching on reconciliation with preparation for reception of the Lord's Supper. Here's an example from a document typically read a week before one receives the Lord's Supper:

> Let us also examine our love, both for God and our neighbors. Remember the great and first commandment to love the Lord our God with all our heart, soul, mind, and strength. Let us consciously determine to live a life of loving service to him, through Christ our Lord. Let us also search ourselves to determine whether we love our neighbors as Christ commands. Do we unselfishly live for the welfare of others? Do our lives reflect the godly virtues of obedience, fidelity, integrity, justice, humility, and contentment? Do we seek reconciliation with our neighbors in all cases of offense?[19]

Here's another example: "Since Christ, by his death, resurrection and ascension has obtained for us the life-giving Spirit who unites us all in one body, we should receive the Lord's Supper in brotherly love, mindful of the communion of saints."[20]

Growing up in the church, I heard those exhortations frequently. As a pastor, I have read many like them to the congregations I have served. Consequently, there have been times when I discouraged members of my congregations from participating in the Lord's Supper. There have also been times when I did not fellowship at the Lord's table or I served the elements to others while not receiving them for myself. I guess you could say that I did not receive the Lord's Supper because I didn't complete my homework. To some, that approach to the Lord's Supper may sound puritanical. I counter that it has everything to do with the unity of the family of God. It flows from the conviction that table fellowship with people is best when shared with those with whom we have been reconciled. In

---

19. "Preparatory Exhortation," 976–77.
20. "The Order for the Sacrament of the Lord's Supper," 64.

such instances, our eating with someone indicates friendship, solidarity, and hospitality.

My father once illustrated that principle for me. As a relatively young man, husband, and father of five children, he suffered a heart attack. It was followed with surgery. While in the hospital, he did not receive the customary visit from his pastor, nor did he expect one, since the pastor was on vacation. An elder of the church filled in admirably by visiting dad before surgery. The Scriptures were read and prayer so offered that my mom and dad quietly rested in the promises of the Lord, the great physician. However, a few days after his surgery, my father learned that the pastor, during his vacation, had visited another member of the church who had been hospitalized at the same time as my dad—and in the very same hospital. This angered my dad and surely didn't help his recovery. He held on to the anger for a few weeks, but then faced a dilemma. The Lord's Supper would be served the coming Sunday, and he knew that he could not participate in the Lord's Supper until he reconciled with the pastor. So my father, a man of few words, drove to the pastor's home on a Saturday morning and initiated a conversation which led to reconciliation. The pastor, who knew about my father's feelings, greeted him with open arms and thanked my father for taking the first step toward reconciliation. The pastor even noted that he was planning on serving, but not partaking of the Lord's Supper because of the fractured relationship with my father. But the next day, the two broke bread together with the family of God.

You may think that story nice, but not for you. So let's look at the relationship between the unity of the church and table fellowship from another perspective. Have you ever been in a restaurant when a family of twelve walked in the door? If so, did you notice how, instead of sitting at three tables of four—each one separated from the other by about three feet—the family insisted that three tables be drawn together as one? It doesn't make logistical sense! Three separate tables of four would place people in closer proximity to one another, yet the family insists on ONE long table. Why? There is something important about sitting together in one place at one time. Perhaps we can learn from that scenario and ask, "How can we affirm our unity when we gather for worship?" Surely our affirmation of unity will impact the space and the location of the furnishings, if not more.

The affirmation of our unity as a congregation prompts other questions. Should we not gather at the same time? Should not adults and children worship together? Should we have multiple worship activities taking place simultaneously? How does our reception of the Lord's Supper, or practice of baptism, affirm our unity as a church? Have we excluded someone—such as a hearing or sight impaired Christ-follower—from full participation in our services? We ask similar questions when hosting a gathering of the extended family as we do not want anyone to feel or be excluded. If we are so careful in that context, shall we, when gathering for worship, not follow Paul's admonition to make every effort to keep the unity of the Spirit?

A Chosen People

Each Christian may worship the Lord privately, while at work, rest or play. The exercise of corporate worship, however, requires that Christians leave their private lives to form an assembly with other Christians. The first movement of a Sunday service, then, is the gathering of the people. By gathering, we respond to God's invitation to worship Him while in fellowship with others. We receive this invitation through the written Word where we read, "Let us not give up meeting together" (Heb 10:25). We also "hear" it through the inner working of the Holy Spirit who convinces us that we should "go to church." Prompted by the Spirit, we leave our homes, hop in our cars, and travel to our meeting place.

The act of gathering affirms a biblical understanding of the nature of the church. On over hundred occasions in Scripture, the word *church* translates the Greek word *ekklesia,* which, in the first century, was commonly used to refer "to an assembly of citizens called to decide matters of common welfare."[21] In the first century church, then, the word *ekklesia* referred to an actual gathering or concrete assembly of believers. So understood, as the Catholic theologian Hans Küng suggests, "there is no *ekklesia* in the intervals between them."[22] For him, the *ekklesia* is instantiated when gathered *on* Sunday mornings but effectively dissolved when scattered.

But there is another layer of meaning to the word *ekklesia.* In the Greek translation of the Hebrew Old Testament, we discover that the word *ekklesia* translates the Hebrew word *qahal,* a designation for God's assembled people. At the foot of Mount Sinai, for example, Moses

---

21. Clapp, *A Peculiar People,* 80.
22. Küng, *The Church,* 118.

delivered the Ten Commandments to the *qahal*. We may surmise, then, that the *ekklesia* or church is not only a gathered community, but a *qahal* or gathered community which *belongs to the Lord*. When Jesus said, "I will build my Church," then, he was not describing a generic gathering of individuals called together to watch a ball game or vote on candidates in an election. Instead, he was referring to the gathering of the people of God, a people called out of darkness into light so that they may become a chosen people, a royal priesthood, a holy nation, and a people belonging to God (1 Pet 2:9).

This may be a hard concept for Americans to grasp. In the United States, the local church has been defined and understood as a voluntary society of like-minded persons.[23] The New Testament, in contrast, describes the local church as a people chosen by our Triune God. So, which shall it be? More importantly, how does the manner in which we gather reflect the difference between the two views of the church?

Those questions prompt some reflection, perhaps even a comparison to the extended family. For example: who hosts the extended family when they gather to celebrate Christmas at grandma's house? Who welcomes each child and grandchild to the gathering? Who is treated with a special level of respect and admiration? The answer to each of those questions is the same: the grandmother.

Now let's ask this series of questions: Who hosts the Sunday service? Who calls us together for worship? Who receives a special level of respect and admiration? Who welcomes each person who gathers? The answer to those questions is our Triune God. But do both the manner in which we gather, as well as our practices while gathered, clearly reflect our host? If the proverbial un-churched person gathered with your congregation for several weeks, how would that person answer this question: Who hosted the party?

We are the chosen and beloved people of God who gather to worship our Beloved. We belong, body and soul, in life and death, to our Triune God. The fact that we belong to God shapes us. We do not gather as enemies of God, fearful of his retribution for our disobedience. We gather as those loved by the Father, redeemed by the Son, and comforted by the Comforter. We gather with the comfort of those who know they are loved by the one who calls together those gathered. This comfort soothes us when stricken with grief. It consoles us when we sorrow. It

---

23. For more on this subject, see Hamstra, "The Americanization of the Church and Its Pastoral Ministry," and Noll in *Old Religion in a New World The Old Religion*.

inspires us with hope. It encourages us when things go against us. It reassures us in the middle of confusion and uncertainty. It gives us a peace beyond comprehension.

A Visible People

We gather as a visible society of human beings, a group of men and women with names and addresses, "a visible community among other communities."[24] This visible community of sinning saints is the people of God, the bride of Christ, the body of Christ, a temple of the Holy Spirit (1 Cor 3:16). This visible community of Corinthian cliques and Galatian heresies is the chosen people of God. What our Lord left behind, as Lesslie Newbigin pointed out a half century ago, "was not a book, nor a creed, nor a system of thought, nor a rule of life, but a visible community."[25] As Christ-followers, we "cannot live except as a visibly defined and organized body with a continuing structure"[26] Hence, our unity as the people of God is not merely ideal or spiritual; "it is visible, social, organic, effected, revealed, and sealed in the fellowship of the one table."[27]

Yet, we are a broken people. The bride of Christ "who is essentially one is divided; she who is essentially holy is unclean; she who is essentially apostolic forgets her missionary task."[28] Plus, as Jesus himself taught (Matt 7:21–23) and as the Twelve Apostles illustrates, some among us are the real deal while others are faking it. Some are close to the Lord while others are admittedly distant. Some have a relationship with God, others are just religious. Some are sinning saints, while others are just sinners. Some have a hangover from drinking too much the previous night; others look like they have just come off of Mount Sinai, their faces aglow by the Spirit. The hearts of some burn with love for God and neighbor, and the hearts of others are lukewarm.

We may choose to resolve those apparent contradictions by distinguishing between the elect and non-elect, the invisible and visible, the ideal and the real, the properly so-called and improperly so-called, the ineffectually called and effectually called, and so forth and so on. Through

24. Newbigin, *The Household of God*, 19–21.
25. Ibid.
26. Ibid., 76.
27. Ibid., 82–83.
28. Ibid., 91.

such mental gymnastics we attempt to explain away the frailties, faults, follies, and foolishness of the visible, yet one, holy, catholic and apostolic church. But when we go down that rabbit trail, we move away from a pretty clear narrative in Scripture: we are the visible people of God.

While our limited human understanding prohibits us from fully understanding the mystery of the visible church, we may still grapple it. When we do, we realize a very important truth about those who gather for worship: we are a mixed bag of saved and unsaved, elect and non-elect, awakened and non-awakened. Plus, even the saved, elect, and awakened experience both good and bad days. Sometimes we glow like fire and other times we smolder (or even stink) like damp wood in a fire pit. As a result, we, the holy bride of Christ, often act like a Gomer, Hosea's adulterous wife.

The truth that the gathered community is a mixed bag impacts our approach as a people to the corporate worship of our Beloved. John Williamson Nevin, as well as a handful of Puritans who came before him, recognized that the gathered community includes several different types of people—*each of which approaches corporate worship differently.*[29] The first type comprises Christ-followers whose worship matches the aspirations of their hearts. We gather for the purpose of responding to God's love with loving worship, but we do so as sinning saints. We also gather as seasonal saints. By that designation, I refer to the changing dynamics or seasons of our faith. Sometimes we gather for worship while in the summer season, when our faith is ablaze. At other times, we gather for worship while in the winter season, when the Lord seems distant and our hearts are cold. Consequently, sometimes we can't wait to gather with other sinning saints to worship our Beloved but, at other times, we gather out of obligation.

Christ-followers are not the only type of people gathered for worship each week. In nearly every gathered community, we will find those who don't have reason to hope. Some are mere "professors" or "pretenders." Jesus describes these individuals in Matthew 7:21–23. These are the ones who sing "Lord, Lord," but who will not be found in heaven. Bewildered by their eternal destination, they ask, "Didn't we prophecy before the gathered community?" To them, Jesus offers these chilling words: "I never knew you." This group of people poses a problem for the gathered community. As professors of faith who participate in the rituals of the

---

29. See Hamstra, *The Reformed Pastor.*

liturgy, they look just like Christ-followers. Since our Triune God is the only one who can distinguish one from the other, we usually assume that each professor is a Christ-follower. And maybe that's OK. But I have often wondered if there is one telling difference between the two. Doesn't it make sense to expect that Christ-followers will welcome attempts to renew and refresh corporate worship, and that mere professors will tend to resist such measures? It seems to me that Christ-followers will long to respond to the love of God with fresh, authentic, and meaningful worship of their Beloved, while professors will tend to be content with going through the motions of their liturgies. If that is true, how important is it for the spiritual leaders of a congregation to discern the spirit of those who object to attempts to renew worship before giving ear to the objections themselves?

In addition to Christ-followers and false professors, we may safely assume that most gathered communities include at least two additional types of people. One group may be described as open and honest unbelievers. They gather with Christ-followers for any number of reasons, some more honorable than others. Nevertheless, their attendance with the congregation does not flow from a regenerated heart. Some in this group may one day become Christ-followers, but until that time they live openly and honestly as those who have rejected the faith. They have no desire to participate in the liturgy of God's people. While they will go through the motions of standing and sitting when the congregation stands and sits, they remain silent while others sing. While others pray and listen, they daydream. It is important for those who lead the liturgy to recognize the presence of this group. It is also important for those who lead worship not to let this group distract them from the Christ-followers in the congregation. Finally, it is important for all Christ-followers to withhold judgment of such individuals, for only God knows the plans he has for them.

The final type of person who gathers each week with Christ-followers, professors, and unbelievers may be described as those who have not yet become Christ-followers, but within whom the Holy Spirit is already at work. Traditionally, Protestant Christians have referred to this group as "awakened sinners." While they have not yet professed their faith in Christ, the Spirit has begun his gracious work within them. We may even say that they have been born again for they, unlike those who have no place for God (Rom 3:10–18), have experienced the working of the Spirit in their souls. Consequently, as God's people worship, they begin to feel harmony among their parts. When the Word is spoken, they hear God speaking directly to them. When worship is offered, they "get it." When fellowship is enjoyed, they are drawn in.

John Nevin is one of many writers who have encouraged pastors and congregations to assume the presence of awakened sinners in every service:

> It should be taken for granted that there are always such persons in his congregation, and he should not think that they are to be found only during commotions. Wherever the Gospel is preached faithfully, there is always an inquiring party, especially among the young, holding a middle position between the obedient and the callous. They should be regarded as a standing class.

The assumption of the presence of the "awakened" among those gathered encourages those who plan worship. Most importantly, it assures us of the presence of seekers whose spiritual thirst can only be quenched by the Lord. It relieves us of the responsibility of drawing these same people into the presence of God for the Spirit, at work within them, has already begun that work. It discourages us from employing manipulative techniques to persuade seekers to accept a spiritual prescription for their souls, for the Holy Spirit has already begun to guide them into life and truth.

Over my years in the ministry, recognizing those categories of individuals among the gathered community has proven helpful. First, it reminds me to refrain from passing judgment on the spiritual life of a person based on superficial observations. The one who prophecies may be a pretender, and the one who looks like a deer transfixed on headlights, may be a seeker. The one who lifts her hands in praise may be in the summer season of the Christian life, and the one who lip-syncs the songs may be in the winter season or dark night of the soul.[30]

Second, it helps me recognize that those gathered may not share the same motivation to attend a Sunday service. Genuine Christ-followers gather for corporate worship as forgiven sinners. We come weary in need of rest, weak in need of strength, and broken in need of healing. Our Sunday suits and hats may suggest otherwise, but we know the truth: we are sinning saints. So, as the outstanding New Testament scholar N.T. Wright writes,

---

30. In *Religious Affections*, Edwards identifies criteria for discerning the gracious operation of the Spirit in a person, most of which do not overlap with the external enthusiasms of the revivalists.

> We come into the presence of Almighty God and feast at his table, not because we are good people, but because we are forgiven sinners. We come, as we come to a doctor, not because we are all well but because we are all sick. We come, not because we've got it all together, but because God's got it all together and has invited us to join him. We come, not because our hands are full of our own self-importance or self-righteousness, but because they are empty and waiting to receive his love, his body and blood, his own very self.[31]

For others, like the professors, corporate worship serves other purposes. Worship attendance could be a religious habit which relieves them of guilt or pacifies a loved one.

Finally, the diverse constituency of the gathered community creates optimism for those who plan and lead worship. We know that, by the power of the Holy Spirit already at work, the liturgy will be embraced by both Christ-followers and awakened sinners. We also know that it will be a spiritually formative experience for those involved. We also know that a percentage of those gathered will resist engaging in the liturgy or reject any and all attempts at liturgical renewal. This will not surprise us. After all, why would a spiritually dead person want a living liturgy offered to a Living God?

A Baptized People

The ritual of baptism more often than not takes place during a congregation's weekly gathering. While it takes place in a corporate environment, it is often understood as an individual or personal experience. In common parlance, baptism has but one layer of meaning, that given it by Peter on Pentecost: personal salvation. With that limitation, baptism in Christ parallels rather than transcends John the Baptist's baptism of repentance and forgiveness of sins (Luke 3:3).

Baptism understood within the whole of the New Testament, however, has multiple layers of meaning. While a sign of cleansing or forgiveness, it is also a sign that one belongs to Jesus, in whose name we are baptized.[32] Furthermore, since we are baptized by one Spirit into one body (1 Cor 12:13), it is also a sign that one belongs to the body of

---

31. Wright, *For All God's Worth*, 79.
32. See Wilken, *The Spirit of Early Christian Thought*.

Christ, the church. Baptism is our membership card in the family of God. Clearly, this does not mean that everyone who has been baptized has received the gift of eternal life, but it does mean that just about everyone who has received the gift of eternal life is baptized. Inasmuch as it is a participation in the death, burial, and resurrection of Jesus, baptism at once signifies the death of the old, unregenerate person, and the emergence of a consecrated new life. Peter calls it the "answer of a good conscience toward God" (1 Pet 3.18).

More importantly for this conversation, baptism in the New Testament is a corporate experience. We are baptized by someone, in obedience to Jesus, the head of the Church, in the name of Jesus, as well as the Father and the Spirit (Matt 28:19), into the body of Christ. This means, as Hans Küng wrote years ago,

> Baptism is never just an individual act concerning Christ and the (person) baptized. This is so because a person does not baptize him (or herself). He or (she) is baptized in the presence of the community, for the community, and by being baptized, (the one baptized) becomes a member of the community. Baptism is entry into this people.[33]

From such an understanding we may conclude that the ritual of baptism is seldom practiced apart from the gathered community. Only in special circumstances would that be the case, an example of such is the baptism of the Ethiopian eunuch (Acts 8:38).

A Diverse People

The mission of God is to create a chosen people with representatives from every tribe and language and people and nation. In his covenant with Abraham, the Lord said, "I will make you into a great nation and I will bless you; I will make your name great, and you will be a blessing . . . and all peoples on earth will be blessed through you" (Gen 12:1–3).[34] In Isaiah 19 God reaffirms his commitment to create a diverse people: "In that day there will be a highway from Egypt to Assyria. The Assyrians will go to Egypt and the Egyptians to Assyria. The Egyptians and Assyrians will worship together. In that day Israel will be the third, along with Egypt and Assyria, a blessing on the earth. The Lord Almighty will bless them,

33. Küng, *The Church*, 273.
34. See Christopher Wright, *The Mission of God*.

saying, "Blessed be Egypt my people, Assyria my handiwork, and Israel my inheritance" (23–26). In the Apocalypse of John, God leaves little room for doubt concerning his desire for a diverse people. In Revelation 5:9–10, we read that those around the throne of God sing to the Lamb of God with these words: "With your blood you purchased individuals for God from every tribe and language and people and nation. You have made them to be a kingdom and priests to serve our God, and they will reign on the earth." In Revelation 7:9–12 we read:

> After this I looked and there before me was a great multitude that no one could count, from every nation, tribe, people and language, standing before the throne and in front of the Lamb. They were wearing white robes and were holding palm branches in their hands. And they cried out in a loud voice: "Salvation belongs to our God, who sits on the throne, and to the Lamb." All the angels were standing around the throne and around the elders and the four living creatures. They fell down on their faces before the throne and worshiped God, saying: "Amen! Praise and glory and wisdom and thanks and honor and power and strength be to our God for ever and ever. Amen!"

Finally, as Rich Mouw observes, Revelation 21 offers a portrait of the multicultural redeemed community by drawing attention to the activity of the kings of the earth:

> I did not see a temple in the city, because the Lord God Almighty and the Lamb are its temple. The city does not need the sun or the moon to shine on it, for the glory of God gives it light, and the Lamb is its lamp. The nations will walk by its light, and the kings of the earth will bring their splendor into it. On no day will its gates ever be shut, for there will be no night there. The glory and honor of the nations will be brought into it. Nothing impure will ever enter it, nor will anyone who does what is shameful or deceitful, but only those whose names are written in the Lamb's book of life (22–27).[35]

Of course, Jesus Christ is the key to the accomplishment of the mission of God. God the Father sent his one and only Son to be the Savior of the world (John 3:16). Jesus announced his intention to seek and save the lost, both Jew and Gentile alike (Luke 19:10). He then wrapped up his ministry on earth by commissioning his ambassadors, the apostles, to make disciples of all nations (Matt 28:19–20), and by empowering his

---

35. Mouw, *He Shines in All That's Fair*.

HOW THE BELOVED SHAPES THE PEOPLE WHO WORSHIP   75

apostles for mission with the gift of the Holy Spirit (Mark 16:9–20, Luke 24:48–53).

We could add to this short list of citations from scripture, but clearly, the mission of God has always been to create a diverse people.[36] As the beloved children of God, we long for the fulfillment of God's mission, even as we pray "May your kingdom come." We look forward to that day when followers of Jesus from every tribe and language and people and nation gather before the Lord in perpetual praise. Until that day, let us commit ourselves, as both individuals and local congregations, to the mission of God. But, let us do so, as Justo Gonzalez implores,

> Not because our community is becoming multicultural, but because heaven will be multicultural; not just to make people of other cultures feel more at home among us, but so that we feel more at home in God's future; not out of some moral or ethical obligation, but "because our eyes have seen the glory of the coming of the Lord, because we know and believe that on that great waking-up morning, when the stars begin to fall, when we gather at the river where angel feet have trod, we shall all, from all nations and tribes and peoples and languages, we shall all sing without ceasing: "Holy, Holy, Holy! All the saints adore thee! Casting down our golden crowns before the glassy sea; cherubim and seraphim; Japanese and Swahili; American and European, Cherokee and Ukrainian; falling down before thee, who were, and art, and evermore shall be!"[37]

If God's mission is to create a diverse people, how does our gathering reflect or live into that future? Minimally, we will embrace an appreciation for the beauty of diversity. But will we take strategic steps to embrace the beauty of diversity? Here's one often overlooked strategy: congregational songs which reflect the diversity a congregation hopes to experience. Here's what I mean: take a look at the authors of your congregational songs and determine if they represent a diverse group of artists. Do they represent generational, racial, ethnic, and gender diversity?

I came to that strategy at a time when many white, American, suburban, Protestant (WASP) congregations embraced God's mission and began pursuing diversity as a congregation. They began to dream about

---

36. See, as examples, Hovda, "Pentecost: Distinctive Cultures and Common Prayer," Dominy, "Spirit, Church, and Mission," and Fernandez, "From Babel to Pentecost."

37. Gonzalez, *The Healing of the Nations*, 112.

how they could better reflect God's plan for a people of many tribes and nations. Consequently, they planned and executed strategic measures to reach that goal. Yet, upon closer examination, I discovered that, in most cases, the music chosen for congregational worship was not diverse. Instead, most had been written by the dominant people group: WASP males just like me. But how does such a practice lovingly advance the mission of God to create a diverse people? Does not love for God prompt a desire to advance the mission of God by selecting congregational songs which reflect the diversity a congregation hopes to experience?

Conclusion

So much more could have been written. I could have, for example, reflected on how the Biblical metaphors of the church—such as Body and Bride—crystallize ways in which our Beloved shapes us as a people. I could have written about how adoption into the family of God transforms us from individuals afflicted by xenophobia (fear of strangers) to a community characterized by philoxenia (love of the stranger). But it is hoped that what has been written suffices to show that in the church, our Triune God has succeeded in his mission of creating a peculiar people—royal and priestly—out of the diverse multitudes of the earth. We worship with the realization that at Pentecost, Israel has merged with Assyria and Egypt. For believers, oneness in worship carries deep implications for our identity, our practices, and our understanding of those around us. We are, in the final accounting, ensconced in a paradox: while church ties may seem fluid and we succumb to the temptation to treat our Sunday gathering like a voluntary society, the redeemed *ekklesia* of God is bound together by cords stronger than race, gender, class, age, or blood.

chapter 5

HOW THE BELOVED SHAPES THE PRACTICES OF WORSHIP

Now it is time to let the proverbial rubber hit the road and discuss the actual activity of worship. The fundamental question before us is, "How may lovers express their love for their Beloved through worship?" Another way of asking the same question is, "What are the essential components of Christian worship?" With those questions I realize, with Susan White, that I run the risk of reducing worship to a collection of bits and pieces to be analyzed.[1] Surely, I don't want to diminish worship in that way. At the same time, I acknowledge that particular practices or actions constitute the "overall pattern and texture" of worship.[2] In other words, worship exists in praxis, not speculation. In order to worship authentically, then, we need to identify, understand, and implement specific practices.

Before diving into a survey of worship practices, I offer a few general remarks. First, in this chapter I will describe transcultural worship practices. I borrow that word and its definition from the *Nairobi Statement on Worship and Culture Contemporary Challenges and Opportunities,* a document produced by the Lutheran World Federation's Study Team on Worship and Culture. This team met in Nairobi in January of 1996 and developed four central principles of the dynamic relationship between worship and culture:

---

1. White, *Foundations of Christian Worship*, 27.
2. Ibid.

1. It is transcultural, the same substance for everyone everywhere, beyond culture.

2. It is contextual, varying according to the local situation (both nature and culture).

3. It is counter-cultural, challenging what is contrary to the Gospel in a given culture.

4. It is cross-cultural, making possible sharing between different local cultures.[3]

In this chapter, I identify and describe six transcultural worship practices. As such, we find these practices wherever and whenever we find Christians loving God through worship. These transcultural practices are praise, prayer, confession, giving, discipline, and recollection. The specifics and logistics of each practice may vary, but we will find the substance of each one in the lives of those who love their Beloved. The words attached to each practice may vary, but we will find each one shaped by Scripture. They are transcultural and have been around for a millennia, practiced by luminaries like Abraham, Moses, David, Mary, the apostles, the martyrs, and countless Christ-followers since them.

Second, I affirm that "practice makes perfect." Just as practice perfects the performance of a pianist, so these practices, in a manner of speaking, perfect our faith. In other words, worship practices shape us. As James K.A. Smith notes, they are "routines and rituals that inscribe particular ongoing habits into our character, such that they become second nature to us."[4] This means that as we love the Lord through worship, we become both better lovers and better worshipers. Conversely, if we worship, intentionally or unintentionally, in a manner that subverts biblical ideals, our spiritual formation will be hindered.

Third, some worship practices shape us more powerfully than others, that is, they carry more weight than others. Liturgical scholars describe this reality by distinguishing between thick and thin practices. Thin practices, like congregational announcements, have but one or two layers of meaning, the most important of which is affirmation of the corporate dimension of the worshiping congregation. Thick practices, like the Lord's Supper, involve multiple layers of meaning. They are "meaning-laden, identity-forming practices that subtly shape us precisely because

---

3. *Nairobi Statement*, 1.3.
4. Smith, *Desiring the Kingdom*, 80.

HOW THE BELOVED SHAPES THE PRACTICES OF WORSHIP

they grab hold of our love."[5] Love prompts many thick practices, the first of which is praise.

Love Prompts Praise

We praise the people we love. In the same way, we shower our Beloved with affirmation for his greatness, goodness, mercy, grace, and love. We acknowledge our Beloved as "the only source of virtue, justice, holiness, wisdom, truth, power, goodness, mercy, life, and salvation;" we "ascribe and render to him the glory of all that is good!"[6] We pay homage to our Beloved "in worship of his person and in thanksgiving for his favors and blessings."[7] As a gathered community, we "exalt His name together" (Ps 34:3). With one voice we "declare the praises of the one who has called us out of darkness into His marvelous light" (1 Pet 2:9).

The content of our praise may be as minimal as a simple "Hallelujah," or "Praise the Lord," or "I Love You, Lord." But normally we choose to praise God by joyfully describing that which prompts our praise, which is to say, we distinguish our God from other gods. We specify the manner in which our Triune God has blessed us and enumerate the attributes which prompt our praise. Like the children of Israel who passed through the water on dry ground and witnessed the destruction of their enemies, we may say:

> I will sing to the Lord, for he is highly exalted. Both horse and driver he has hurled into the sea. The Lord is my strength and my defense; he has become my salvation. He is my God, and I will praise him, my father's God, and I will exalt him (Exod 15:1–2).

Or like A.W. Tozer, who, in his classic work *The Knowledge of the Holy*, reflects on the nearly two dozen praise-worthy attributes of God, we may carefully articulate the variety of characteristics which constitute the majesty of our Lord.

Those saved by the cross of Christ long for an opportunity to praise the Lord. As guilty sinners saved by grace and indwelt by the Holy Spirit, our hearts burst forth in gratitude. We long to "waste our time immersed

---

5. Smith, *Desiring the Kingdom*, 83.
6. Calvin, *The Necessity of Reforming the Church*, 16.
7. Stanton, "Praise," 865.

in all the fullness of God's splendor."[8] With the Psalmist we proclaim, "Better is one day with God's people in praise, than a thousand days elsewhere" (Ps 84:10).

God does not leave us without coaching on how to love him with our praise. Psalm 100 encourages us to worship the Lord with joy and gladness. It also teaches us to blend reverence and fear with shouting and singing. While looking for an example of such worship, we find that Mary, the mother of Jesus, couples humility with praise. While responding to God's grace she readily acknowledges her undeserving place in the history of redemption (Luke 1). We find much of the same in Hannah's prayer, the "Magnificat of the Old Testament" (I Sam 2). In Psalm 145, we read how David looks beyond the gifts to the Giver. He thanks the Lord for the gifts the Lord has showered upon him and praises the Lord for his greatness, goodness, glory, and grace.

Through praise we express our love for the Lord God, our Beloved. We may consider corporate praise a thick practice with as many as four additional layers of meaning. First, corporate praise unifies the body of Christ. E. Byron Anderson writes, "As a practice by which persons express personal and communal faith, hymn singing physically and mentally situates the person in a context of relatedness to the whole of a community whose voice is united in song and to God."[9] Second, praise heals the hearts of worshipers by confirming the faith and soothing the hearts of believers.[10] At times we struggle to believe that which we profess through praise, but the praise of God shapes and strengthens our faith. By singing "Great is Thy Faithfulness," for example, we find it easier to believe, in good times and bad, that our God is faithful. It is as if the lyrics of the hymn carve an interior landscape of trust and gratitude. At other times, praise soothes the hearts of worshipers by sparking memories of significant moments in our spiritual journey. While such singing may prompt tears, it also facilitates healing. Anderson has observed, "The singing of a hymn is more than making music, more than a nice song filling dead space in a liturgy, more than an aesthetic act, more than an act of self-expression. It is an act of pastoral care in times of need and rejoicing."[11]

---

8. Dawn, *A Royal "Waste" of Time*, 343.
9. Anderson, "O for a heart to praise my God," 12.
10. Carothers, *Power in Praise*, 1–18
11. Anderson, "O for a heart to praise my God," 11.

Third, praise sanctifies us.[12] On over fifty occasions in the Psalms alone, God commands his people to worship him. Worship, then, may be viewed as an act of obedience. God calls us to praise him whether we feel like it or not. As we submit our wills to the Lord's through obedience we mature in the faith. Plus, during corporate worship we are "stirred up to more and more genuine devotion to God."[13] Fourth, praise confirms our identity as a people created in the image of God. As the Westminster Confession states, we have been created by God to glorify and enjoy him forever. By praising the Lord, we embrace our identity. Our worship—prayers, gifts, praise—is an offering to the Lord (Acts 10:4). They are as incense on the golden altar before the throne of God (Rev 8:5).

Love Prompts Prayer

I once served a congregation that held a mid-week prayer meeting. Each Wednesday night, a couple dozen church members gathered for a time of prayer led by the pastor. During my tenure, the prayer meeting was seldom well attended, when compared to the number of those who attended Sunday morning services. That fact didn't please the unofficial elders of the congregation who measured the congregation's spiritual maturity, not by how many came to Sunday morning service, or by how many who attended the Sunday evening service, but by how many came to the mid-week prayer meeting. In response to the weak attendance, the faithful attendees encouraged me to offer a Sunday sermon on the importance of attending the mid-week prayer meeting, but I couldn't find a text to go with that sermon.

Truth be told, I wasn't a big fan of the mid-week prayer meeting. My primary objection was that we didn't pray much during the "prayer meeting." The weekly mid-week service lasted sixty minutes. That time was filled with a couple songs, a thirty minute lesson from Scripture, audible prayer requests for those suffering from any number of medical conditions, and a few minutes of "popcorn" prayer. My second objection was that it seemed to me that the real prayer meeting of the congregation took place every Sunday morning. Our weekly liturgy included prayers of praise, thanksgiving, confession, intercession, and petition. Those prayers were offered in several modes, including unison readings, silence,

12. Rice and Huffstutler, *Reformed Worship*, 195.
13. Old, *Worship Reformed According to Scripture*, 46.

the traditional pastoral prayer, and praise. In fact, we spent as much time in prayer as we did listening to the sermon. My third objection was that the weekly gathering or Sunday service is the most fitting time for God's people to pray as a people. It is then that most of the congregation gathers. It is then that, as Dallas Willard notes, prayer can shape our theology as well as clarify and reframe our convictions.[14]

Prayer, broadly considered, is communication with God—communication understood "as meaningful, interactive self-disclosure."[15] As Christ-followers, we love the Lord and long to communicate with him. Towards that end, we employ different types of prayer, including confession, intercession, and supplication. But lest our prayers suffer from the "gimme" syndrome, we work hard to balance our petitions with prayers of thanksgiving and adoration. With our prayers of thanks, we highlight the many blessings God has poured into our lives, but love will not let us to stop there. We must praise the Lord; it is an ontological necessity. After having received God's manifold gifts of mercy and grace, we long to praise the giver of the gifts, our Beloved Triune God. While tempted, we don't want to be so enthralled with the gifts that we forget to praise the giver of every good and perfect gift (Jas 1:17). We hope that our "We thank you for" gives way to countless variations of Psalm 63:

> You, God, are my God, earnestly I seek you;
> I thirst for you, my whole being longs for you,
> in a dry and parched land where there is no water.
> I have seen you in the sanctuary and beheld your power and your glory.
> Because your love is better than life, my lips will glorify you.
> I will praise you as long as I live, and in your name I will lift up my hands.
> I will be fully satisfied as with the richest of foods;
> with singing lips my mouth will praise you.

Praise, then, is a form of prayer. While we don't classify every prayer as an act of worship, we may conclude that every act of praise is a prayer. As a form of prayer, our praise suffers from predictable maladies, one of which is vain glory.[16] Like the Pharisees, our prayers can become opportunities to spread our wings like a peacock. Another is insincerity. Forgetting Jesus' scathing words to the Pharisees (Matt 23), we occasionally

---

14. Willard, *The Great Omission*, 95.

15. Howard, *Introduction to Christian Spirituality*, 300.

16. Diogenes, among others in the early church, includes vain glory in his "eight thoughts" which would attack the earnest Christian.

go through the motions—lip synching our praise with little thought or passion. We string together pious sounding words and call it a prayer of praise without ever thinking about the implications of our words for, if we did, our entire demeanor would be changed.

Over nearly thirty-five years of pastoral ministry, I have made many mistakes in my public prayer ministry. The biggest mistake was my failure to prepare my prayers. Consequently, they became rote, stale, and repetitious. On some occasions I even offered words inconsistent with my theological convictions. Thankfully, somewhere along the line, a fellow pastor made this observation: "In most of our worship services, we pray as much as we preach, but how much time do we commit to preparing our prayers?" That question struck a nerve. I had been trained to spend ten to twenty hours a week preparing one sermon, but I occasionally ran into the pulpit and prayed extemporaneously. Now, I write and read most of my prayers.

Like many pastors, I find inspiration from the prayers of others. Sometimes I borrow their prayers, giving credit where credit is due. Or I scan a book of prayers, like George Appleton's *Oxford Book of Prayer*, until I find a prayer that fits the liturgy. I then paraphrase it or build upon it. In the process I have discovered that such preparation allows me to lead pray with sincerity while keeping my prayers fresh and unpredictable, two important qualities for long-term resident pastors. Plus, it has improved my ability to prayer extemporaneously. All things considered, reading the prayers of those who have gone before me has been one of the more important disciplines of my pastoral ministry.

Love Prompts Confession

Love not only prompts praise for the Beloved, it also prompts confession of sin. The prophet Isaiah illustrates the connection between the two. After his encounter with the glory of God, Isaiah cried out, "I am ruined, for I am a man of unclean lips, and I live among a people of unclean lips, and my eyes have seen the King, the Lord God Almighty (Isa 6:5). The sequence in Isaiah 6 includes three distinct movements. First, we worship the Lord whose majesty and holiness and greatness no person can measure. By this act we become more aware of the glory and wholly-otherness of God.[17]

---

17. Piper, *Desiring God*, 46–48.

Second, the light of God's grandeur illumines our shortcomings and deficiencies. Once again we see ourselves as God sees us. John Calvin writes:

> It is certain that a man never achieves clear knowledge of himself unless he has first looked upon God's face, and then descends from contemplating him to scrutinize himself. For we always seem to ourselves righteous and upright and wise and holy—this pride is innate in all of us . . . As long as we do not look beyond the earth, being quite content with our own righteousness, wisdom, and virtue, we flatter ourselves most sweetly, and fancy ourselves all but demigods.[18]

Jonathan Edwards referred to the proper attitude of the worshiper as "evangelical humility." He believed that the true worship of God not only convicts the conscience, but produces a "change of inclination affecting the whole self."[19] It transforms the worshiper into a seeker, receptive to the transforming work of the Holy Spirit. It puts us where our loving Lord wants us to be: in a place of humble dependence, with open arms to receive his grace.

Third, we seek reconciliation with the Lord. The conviction of sin draws us to the throne of grace where we hope to find forgiveness from the Lord whose grace is greater than our sin. Once again, Isaiah provides the example. After his encounter with the holiness and glory of God, Isaiah cries out, "I am ruined, for I am a man of unclean lips, and I live among a people of unclean lips, and my eyes have seen the King, the Lord God Almighty (Isa 6:5). He wants assurance that his "guilt is taken away" and "sin atoned for" (6–7). Like Isaiah, "the more we encounter the holy God in our worship, the more we recognize our utter sinfulness and are driven to repentance."[20] Donald Bloesch concurs:

> Worship that is done in spirit and in truth will entail an encounter with the Holy, who includes and transcends moral goodness. A true encounter with the Holy precipitates a sense of awe in which we experience our helplessness and littleness before an almighty God.[21]

---

18. Calvin, *Institutes of the Christian Religion*, I.1.ii.

19. "Evangelical Humility" is the sixth of twelve signs of "genuine gracious affection" described by Edwards in *Religious Affections*, 35.

20. Dawn, *Reaching Out Without Dumbing Down*, 90.

21. Bloesch, *The Church*, 119.

For this reason, then, those gathered for worship desire a prayer of confession. A service without such leaves true worshipers longing for more.

The prayer of confession may take one of several forms. We may sing it through the use of a hymn or read it in unison. We may offer a specific prayer in silence. We may even confess our sins by proxy, affirming as our own the spoken prayer of the pastor or the prayer sung by the choir or soloist. When we pray, we may assume a physical position of humility before the Lord. We may sit with bowed head, a medieval sign of submission to one's Lord. We may kneel before the Lord or we may follow the ancient custom of holding our hands flat together. Whatever our posture, it will reflect humble submission before the Lord.

Naturally, an announcement of the Gospel follows our confession of sin. Traditionally, this element has been called "absolution." Once convicted of alienation from God, we need assurance of reconciliation. Once convinced of our sins, we need affirmation of our forgiveness. More specifically, we need to hear the Gospel. This is not the occasion for the liturgist or pastor to offer personal words of encouragement. We have sinned against the Lord and only a word from the Lord will do. So the worship leader, in the name of Jesus, best read a selection from God's Word which captures the good news of reconciliation. He or she best offer a public declaration that our sins are forgiven through Jesus Christ.

The assurance of forgiveness often leads to a desire for more worship on the part of those assured. We witness the connection between the two in Jesus' conversation with a Pharisee named Simon (Luke 7:36–50). While dining in his home, a "woman who had lived a sinful life" cleaned Jesus' feet, kissed them, and anointed them with perfume. Simon objected to such a lavish act of adoration. His objection led Jesus to compare the actions of the woman to those of the Pharisee. Jesus noted that when he came to Simon's home, he did not wash the feet of Jesus or even greet him with a kiss, but the "sinful" woman had kissed his feet incessantly. Jesus explained to Simon that the woman loved Jesus because she had a profound conviction of sin and a deep assurance of forgiveness. It was this love that prompted her adoration. In the same way, our reconciliation with the Lord—the acknowledgment of sin, a prayer of confession, and the assurance of forgiveness—prompts loving praise to the Lord.

Love Prompts Gifts

Debbie and I have had the privilege of watching our four children unite their hearts and lives as one in marriage. Each relationship began differently but each led to marriage. Each relationship included a dating process ornamented by the ritual of gift-giving, a popular love language.[22] Now that they are married, that ritual continues. Simple observation leads me to conclude that love requires it.

Centuries before Moses litigated the tithe, Abraham illustrated how the beloved of God respond to grace with gratitude. In Genesis 14 we read that Abraham defeated King Kedorlaomer and his allies in order to retrieve his nephew Lot, a prisoner of war. After his victory, Abraham traveled to Jerusalem, then known as Salem, where he gratefully gave the servant of God Melchizedek ten percent of the spoils of war. Abraham's experience has been replicated in countless lives throughout the history of the Church. Touched by the Spirit and moved by grateful hearts, God's children express their love for their Beloved by offering financial or material gifts. What else would inspire and stimulate:

- The patriarchs to give a tenth of their possessions to the Lord (Gen 28:22)?
- The Macedonians to give well beyond their means (2 Cor 8:5)?
- Zaccheus to give half of his proceeds to the Lord (Luke 19:8)?
- The widow to give nearly all she had to the Lord (Mark 12:41)?
- A woman to pour expensive ointment on the head of Jesus (Mark 14:3–9)? and
- Christ to humble himself in the form of a servant, suffer, and die (Phil 2:5–8)?

Love offers the only explanation for those radical acts of gratitude, as well as others recorded throughout the Scriptures. Love offers the only motivation powerful enough to separate a person's possessions from his or her hands. Lovers, it seems, find words insufficient and therefore compliment them with actions. They decide to share with others, build others up, and prioritize the Beloved over self through visible, touchable acts. Love gives. Love shares. Love reflects itself in selfless action and sacrificial giving.

---

22. Chapman, *The 5 Love Languages*.

But what do we give someone who has it all? What do we give God who has no need of anything? Who owns the cattle on a thousand hills (Ps 50:9–12)? The apostle Paul suggests that we give the Lord our lives as living sacrifices (Rom 12:1). But even that is not enough for lovers. So we give something tangible—the first fruits of the harvest.

There are many motivations for giving money to the Lord. We may give for tax advantages. We may give for the survival of our local church. We may give out of guilt or embarrassment. We may give out of a spirit of obligation. We may give because congregational receipts are behind budget. Each one of those motives, however, falls short of the ideal. The best motivation is a thankful and loving heart. When love motivates us, we give cheerfully, which explains why God loves a cheerful giver (2 Cor 9:6–7). When love moves us, as it did the widow who gave two mites, our giving is an act of worship (Mark 12:41).

Each week the liturgy of the weekly gathering provides an opportunity for believers to express love and devotion to their Beloved through giving. Some congregations have removed this practice from the liturgy, leaving those gathered with the impression that love doesn't give or, worse yet, that God's love doesn't prompt acts of gratitude. Reconciled Christ-followers know better. Like the woman who perfumed the feet of Jesus, we gather each week to pour our praise on the Lord. That praise will include our songs, but also include the perfume in our alabaster jars. It must include such. There is no stopping us from giving back to him who has given us so much.

While we may offer such gifts at any time, the weekly gathering of God's people typically includes an opportunity for such an action. We have biblical precedent for this practice. In the Old Testament, we read that material or financial sacrifices characterized the regular worship of God's people. When we examine the New Testament church, we learn that the perfect sacrifice of Christ did not encourage Christians to change that practice. Instead, in I Corinthians 16:2 we read, "On the first day of every week (planned), each one of you (personal) should set aside a sum of money in keeping with his income" (proportionate). So, following the example of the Old Testament, we consider financial or material gifts an act of worship, and following the example of the Corinthians, we practice personal, planned, and proportionate giving. We do so while recognizing that our gifts are meant to reflect an encompassing gift, that of our lives.

We refer to this worship practice as an "offering." That word implies "something freely given, something presented as a token of dedication or devotion." The purpose of the offering is "to give our first fruits to God, to render to God a sacrifice of praise."[23] The meaning of the offering may be symbolized by an offertory procession, during which worshipers present their gifts to God with prayers of dedication and songs of gratitude.

The Bible offers specific direction for this act of worship. First, we should resist the temptation to follow the example of the Pharisees and turn this practice into one of self-promotion. We may accomplish this goal by offering our gifts secretly, thereby refraining from announcing to others how much we give to the Lord (Matt 6:1–4). This practice requires some practice for secrecy, as Willard notes, is itself a spiritual discipline.[24] Second, we should resist methods of receiving gifts which fail to reinforce the seven-fold unity of the congregation (Eph 4:4–6). The reception of the offering should not divide the congregation into tithers and the non-tithers, those who give a lot and those who give a little, those who have and those who have not. Third, we should practice joyful generosity since "God loves a cheerful giver" (2 Cor 9:5–6). For some Christians, this means applauding the announcement of the offering, because clapping is typically associated with joy in American culture. On a deeper level, the volitional act of clapping engenders a spirit of cheer. Fourth, we should give sacrificially. This thread of teaching runs throughout the Scriptures. In the Old Testament, God instructs his people selecting animals for sacrifices to pick the best, not the broken and maimed. In the New Testament, Jesus lifts up, as an example for us all, the sacrificial giving of the poor, like that of an impoverished widow (Mark 12:41–43).

In many churches, ushers or deacons or other appointed persons collect the offerings and present them to the Lord on behalf of the people. In other settings, worshipers leave their seats and process to a predetermined location where they deposit their offerings. In most cases a prayer accompanies the offering, either before or after. One popular pattern is to begin the offering with an announcement and invitation to give, and then close the offering with a prayer of dedication.

The offering may include other forms of gifts, such as food, clothing, or supplies for a specific need. Congregants may also give of their time and talent through the ministry of music. Children may also offer musical gifts or receive the offering or bring forward signs and symbols of their own gifts to God. The audio-video team might stream announcements

23. *The Worship Sourcebook*, 235–36.
24. Willard, *The Spirit of the Disciplines*, 156–91.

regarding congregational ministries while the offering is being received, thereby communicating that the work of the church is an offering to the Lord. Since the offering is an act of love, there is no end to the manner in which Christians may desire to share their gifts with the Lord.

Love Prompts Discipline

As a child, the longest ten to fourteen days in my life began on Christmas Day and concluded the Sunday after New Year's Day. The Ebenezer Christian Reformed Church (Berwyn, Illinois) of which I was a baptized member, hosted a worship service on Christmas Day, a morning and evening service the Sunday after Christmas, a New Year's Eve service, a New Year's Day service, and a morning and evening service the Sunday after New Year's Day. My faithful, hard-working pastor led most of the services. My faithful parents brought me and my siblings to each one. They, like theirs, believed that each time God's people gather and the Word of God is proclaimed, we received a fresh Word from the Lord—a unique blessing we don't get anywhere else. They also believed that Christians can transform secular holidays into sacred moments to receive such blessings. So, they disciplined themselves to attend as many services as offered.

For centuries, Christians have disciplined themselves to gather with God's people on a weekly basis for a time of worship, fellowship, and more. Typically, they have viewed Sunday as the day for such gatherings. It was on the first day of the week that our Triune God began the process of creation. It was on the first day of the week that God the Father, by the power of the Spirit, raised Jesus Christ, his son, from the grave. It was on the first day of the week that the risen Christ appeared to his disciples (John 20:19–26). It was on the first day of the week that the Holy Spirit fell upon the first church in Jerusalem, so it was on the first day of the week that the church we know was born. We are not surprised to learn, then, that it was on the first day of the week that the "First Church" gathered for worship (Act 20:7). The early Christians viewed the first day of the week as a day of hope and resurrection.[25] So while, for many, the first day of the week may be like any other, for Christians it has traditionally been viewed as a day of remembrance and expectation.[26]

---

25. Allen, "Calendar and Lectionary in Reformed Perspective and History," 397.
26. See Old, *Worship Reformed*, 23–32.

Like those who have come before us, we discipline ourselves to gather weekly for the corporate worship of our Triune God. This weekly pattern has become even more significant for us who now live in a post-Christian context. We can no longer expect to find our faith confirmed—either implicitly or explicitly—by culture. Instead, we can expect to find it severely challenged. Hence, we need to gather regularly, apart from the world, to be formed by the Word and Spirit, if we have any hope to represent Christ in the world. If we are unable to discipline ourselves in such a manner, our love for God will grow lukewarm and our witness to the world will be dulled.

Some Christians deepen their commitment to the Lord's Day by equating it with the Sabbath Day. Like King Charlemagne, they believe that "the Sabbath is the day Christians are to set apart for private and public acts of worship; the Lord's Day is the Christian Sabbath."[27] Other Christians implicitly or explicitly reject Sunday as the Lord's Day, considering "every day alike" (Rom 14:5). Since the early Christians met every day, they believe that they may gather for worship on any day. "Fully convinced in their own minds" that Christ is Lord of all, they don't regard one day as "more special" than another (Rom 14:6).

While some folk discipline themselves to gather weekly with fellow Christians on a day other than Sunday, and while the circumstances of life require some Christians to gather for worship on a day other than Sunday, I suggest we walk cautiously before either rejecting the tradition of Sunday as the Lord's Day or equating the Lord's Day with the Sabbath Day. Instead, when it comes to the relationship between the Lord's Day and the Sabbath, let's thank our Creator for the model of one day of rest every seven days. Let us also affirm that the principle of weekly worship on the Lord's Day rests on a strong biblical tradition. Finally, let us thank the Lord when the circumstances of life allow the Lord's Day and our Sabbath Day to be the same day for that combination has been a special blessing for many people for many years.

Love Prompts Recollection

My grandfather, Andrew Post, was an ice and coal turned ice and oil guy. He delivered blocks of ice to the kitchens of many homes, placing them carefully in their ice boxes. He also delivered bags of cubed ice to

---

27. Hart and Mueller, *With Reverence and Awe*, 63.

restaurants, banquet halls, and drinking establishments. In the winter, when the ice business slowed down, he delivered oil for the furnaces of many of the same homes to which he delivered blocks of ice. By the time I was a teenager, my grandfather's body was starting to break down. All the years of shouldering heavy bags of ice and coal aggravated his hips and he resorted to walking with the aid of a cane. That accessory complicated the logistics of hauling ice. So, near the conclusion of my thirteenth birthday party, my mother offered my services to her father. He wasn't quick to accept my mother's offer, but when I repeated it, he accepted. I began working Saturdays during the school year and Monday through Saturdays in the summer. That arrangement lasted four years, with my brother Don serving as my capable back-up and substitute. When my grandfather passed away in the Lord at the age of seventy, I was devastated. While twenty-two years old and a follower of Jesus at the time of my grandfather's death, I found little solace from the Lord or his people. I was especially aggravated by the levity of those who visited the family the two days before the memorial service. I wanted to see people mourning and stricken with grief, but all I heard was laughter as people shared memorable stories about my grandfather.

I have learned a little bit since my grandfather's death. Among the many lessons learned is this: love recollects. Love prompts memories and memories lead to stories. Love prompts recollection and recollection leads to appreciation, thanksgiving, even praise. Love prompts reflection and reflection leads to renewed commitments to honor the memory of lost love. Love praises the beloved by telling stories of the beloved.

This explains my appreciation for the Lord's Supper, and perhaps it explains yours. Love praises the Beloved by telling stories of the Beloved, and there is no greater story than that told than how God so loved the world that he gave his one and only Son (John 3:16). So, as we share the bread and cup, we praise the Lord by telling the "old, old story of Jesus and his love." We tell the story of our Savior's suffering and death for our sins, that "he was pierced for our transgressions and crushed for our iniquities" (Isa 53:5). We tell the story of our Savior's resurrection by the power of the Holy Spirit. We assure one another of His promises of eternal fellowship and of his return to judge the living and the dead.

We tell this story out of love for our Beloved, but there is more going on than our love for God. The Lord's Supper is a thick practice.[28] By that

---

28. See Cavanaugh, *Theological Imagination*.

I mean that it is "a physical, ritual action, mandated by Jesus, through which God acts to nourish, sustain, comfort, challenge, teach, and assure us."[29] In addition, it is one of the regular practices of the early church. We may summarize the multiple layers of the Lord's Supper in this way: it is a feast of "remembrance, communion, and hope."[30] By eating the bread and drinking the cup, we not only remember our redemption in Jesus Christ through his death on the cross and gain renewed hope for that day when we will enjoy a wedding feast in heaven, but we also commune with Christ (1 Cor 10:17). The nineteenth-century Reformed theologian John Nevin, echoing the sentiments of John Calvin, describes our communion through the Lord's Supper as a "real participation" with Christ.[31] Clarifying his position Nevin writes:

> In the Lord's Supper the believer communicates not only with the Spirit of Christ, or with his divine nature, but with Christ himself in his whole living person; so that he may be said to be fed and nourished by his very flesh and blood.[32]

Personally, I don't understand how Christ is present in the Lord's Supper. I don't understand how he nourishes my soul through the eating of bread and drinking of grape juice. But because the Bible is the inspired word of God, I acknowledge that mystery as true. I believe that participation in the Lord's Supper is communion with Christ, who is my life, light, righteousness, wisdom, knowledge, sanctification, and redemption. Hence, through participation in the Lord's Supper I grow in grace in a way I would not otherwise grow. Through him I become more like him. John Calvin describes that benefit in this way:

> In (the Lord's Supper) we have a witness of our growth into one body with Christ such that whatever is his may be called ours . . . This is the wonderful exchange he has made with us; that, becoming Son of man with us, he has made us sons of God with him; that, by his descent to earth, he has prepared an ascent to heaven for us; that, by taking on our mortality, he has conferred his immortality upon us; that, accepting our weakness, he has strengthened us by his power; that, receiving our poverty unto himself, he has transferred his wealth to us; that, taking the

---

29. *Worship Sourcebook*, 305–306.
30. "Liturgy for the Lord's Supper," 65.
31. Nevin, *The Mystical Presence*, 55.
32. Ibid., 58.

weight of our iniquity upon himself, he has clothed us with his righteousness.[33]

That understanding of the Lord's Supper promotes both decisive preparation by the worshiper and frequent participation. With respect to preparation, we examine ourselves before eating the bread and drinking cup so we do not participate in the sacrament in an "unworthy manner" (1 Cor 11:27-28). We also warn one another that anyone who comes to the table with unrepentant sins "eats and drinks judgment" on him or herself (1 Cor 11:29).

With respect to the frequency of participation, our convictions about the Lord's Supper suggest that we partake frequently, perhaps even weekly. After all, we believe that the Lord's Supper offers grace that we don't typically receive anywhere else, and that through participation in the supper, Christ mystically and really presents himself and his benefits to us.

Ecclesiastical experience has encouraged some to limit the number of times the Lord's Supper is offered. One argument has been that an increased frequency will diminish appreciation for it. Another argument, closely linked to the practice of church discipline, states that the Sacrament is so special that it requires significant preparation, so much so that one could not participate in weekly Communion without "eating and drinking" judgment on self. Congregations of such a mind may offer the Lord's Supper as few as four times a year.

Each congregation must wrestle with the issue of frequency, finding a place at or within the two poles of weekly celebration and quarterly. On one hand, it seems to me that no fault can be found with any congregation that subscribes to the weekly celebration of the Lord's Supper. Such a practice rests on a strong biblical and theological foundation. It also responds to the yearnings of a new generation of Christians who long for visible and sensual elements in worship. On the other hand, those offering the sacrament as infrequently as four times a year seem to stand on shaky ground.

In summary, those planning worship will find a place for the Lord's Supper because love demands it. Love prompts recollection—to "do this in remembrance of me." Plus, we need it. Our faith, like the light of a lantern, diminishes without the oil of God's grace. Our faith, like human bodies, grows faint without nourishment and exercise. Like Peter, we

---

33. Calvin, *Institutes of Christian Religion* IV.17.2.

deny the Lord. Like Thomas, we doubt the Lord. Like Saul and David, we disobey the Lord. Without spiritual nourishment for our souls, the stress and strain of life frays our faith and glazes our love. We need the nourishment of Jesus Christ who is the Bread of Life and who offers the only water that quenches our thirst (John 4:10). Through the operation of the Holy Spirit, coupled with faith, the sacraments nourish our souls and empower our faith. It is by grace we believe and by grace we continue to believe.

Conclusion

How may lovers express their love for their Beloved through worship? Since love is so deep and our Beloved is so great, individuals and groups find countless ways to express their love for the Lord. In this chapter I have identified those practices which are transcultural, that is, those which have been practiced for centuries, throughout the world, by those who love the Lord. These practices include praise, prayer, confession, giving, discipline, and recollection. And as they have been practiced, they have helped worshipers become better lovers and better worshipers.

chapter 6

HOW THE BELOVED SHAPES THE CONTEXT OF WORSHIP

THE TRIUNE GOD WE worship is creating "a chosen people, a royal priesthood, a holy nation" (1 Pet 2:9). He has been about this mission for some time. In Genesis 12:1–3 we read this word from God to Abram, "I will make you into a great nation and I will bless you; I will make your name great, and you will be a blessing... and all peoples on earth will be blessed through you." The mission continued with the arrival of Jesus Christ who came to seek and save the lost (Luke 19:10) and who commissioned his apostles to make disciples from every nation (Matt 28:19–20). The work of making disciples will continue until our Triune God determines it completed. At that point, we, God's special possession, will be escorted into heaven to worship the Lord all of our days. In Revelation 7:9–12 we receive this picture of our eternal destiny:

> After this I looked and there before me was a great multitude that no one could count, from every nation, tribe, people and language, standing before the throne and in front of the Lamb. They were wearing white robes and were holding palm branches in their hands. And they cried out in a loud voice: "Salvation belongs to our God, who sits on the throne, and to the Lamb." All the angels were standing around the throne and around the elders and the four living creatures. They fell down on their faces before the throne and worshiped God, saying: "Amen! Praise and glory and wisdom and thanks and honor and power and strength be to our God for ever and ever. Amen!"

That apocalyptic vision, given to the apostle John, of the completed mission of God confirms that God's plan has always been for a heaven with people from every nation, tribe, people, and language who live in blessed fellowship with one another and with the Lord. As citizens of the world, whose primary enterprise has been war, we long, with repentance, for that day. As citizens of a world plagued by tribalism, nativism, imperialism, ethnic cleansing, and unspeakable forms of barbarism, we long, with repentance, for that day. As the beloved children of God, we long for the fulfillment of his plan for his world. With living hope we look forward to that day when we, with all the saints, worship our Triune God who deserves all honor, glory, and praise.

Until that day we will "declare the praises of him who called (us) out of darkness into his wonderful light" (1 Pet 2:9–10). That is indeed our purpose as a church; everything else flows from that overarching resolution. And until that day, we will worship the Triune God within a particular culture—we cannot escape it. Carl F. H. Henry states that principle eloquently:

> Every human being is born into some cultural context. None of us can choose, moreover, into which cultural setting he or she will emerge to life on earth. Inevitably a cultural given impinges on us. We learn a particular language in a particular historical age. If we move to another country, a different context of humanly shared beliefs, ideals, and institutions await us. Nobody lives in a cultural vacuum except as exiles sealed off from society.[1]

For the time being, then, there is an inseparable relationship between worship and culture. Our worship here on earth will always be "culturally conditioned."[2] Unlike heaven, where disciples from many tribes and nations worship in one context, God's people on earth worship in as many contexts as there are tribes, nations, people, and languages, a reality foreshadowed on the day of Pentecost. These innumerable contexts represent the dramatic, unpredictable, and exciting encounter between worship and culture.

The mention of culture introduces a vast subject and begs for clarification. At its core, however, culture represents the fulfillment of God's mandate to care for creation (Gen 1:27). It is the fruit of our interaction

---

1. Henry, *Twilight of a Great Civilization*, 115.
2. Witvliet, *Worship Seeking Understanding*, 119.

with creation; it is what we make out of creation. As H. Richard Niebuhr noted over a century ago:

> Culture is an artificial, secondary environment which we superimpose on the natural. It comprises language, habits, beliefs, customs, social organizations, inherited artifacts, technical processes, and values.[3]

Our interaction with creation, the environment we superimpose on nature, and the processes which govern our activities include three prominent ingredients. First, culture includes values or principles that influence, shape, and direct the life of a people. To illustrate this point I offer this list of American values from Marian Beane, the Director of the International Student/Scholar Office on the campus of the University of North Carolina in Charlotte.[4] She organized her list of American values for international students preparing to study in the United States.

- *Individuality*: U.S. Americans are encouraged at an early age to be independent and to develop their own goals in life. They are encouraged to not depend (too much) on others including their friends, teachers and parents. They are rewarded when they try harder to reach their goals.
- *Privacy*: U.S. Americans like privacy and enjoy spending time alone. Foreign visitors will find U.S. American homes and offices open, but what is inside the American mind is considered to be private.
- *Equality:* U.S. Americans uphold the ideal that everyone "is created equal" and has the same rights. This includes women as well as men of all ethnic and cultural groups living in the U.S.
- *Time:* U.S. Americans take pride in making the best use of their time. In the business world, "time is money." Being "on time" for class, an appointment, or for dinner with your host family is important.
- *Informality:* The U.S. American lifestyle is generally casual.
- *Achievement & Hard Work/Play:* The foreign visitor is often impressed at how achievement oriented Americans are and how hard they both work and play.

---

3. Niebuhr, *Christ and Culture,* 32. See also Lee, *Marginality,* 52.

4. This extensive quote is included here with permission from the author, Marian Beane.

- *Direct & Assertive:* U.S. Americans try to work out their differences face-to-face and without a mediator. They are encouraged to speak up and give their opinions.

- *Looking to the Future and to Change:* Children are often asked what they want to be "when they grow up"; college students are asked what they will do when they graduate; and professors plan what they will do when they retire. Change is often equated with progress and holding on to traditions seems to imply old and outdated ways.

Americans may read Beane's list with incredulity, thinking such values universal rather than contextual. They would then discover that the values of American culture have so influenced their lives that they mistakenly view their values as universal.

Second, culture includes patterns or predictable and typical ways individuals within a community form concepts, express themselves, and celebrate life together. In North America, one need but survey the greeting card industry to confirm the presence of such practices. While visiting a Hallmark store, you will find more than a dozen different types of cards, including those designed specifically for the celebration or recognition of holidays, birthdays, anniversaries, graduations, the loss of love by death, and more. Taken together, they mirror the patterns by which we share life together.

Third, culture includes institutions or traditional rites by which communities mark the passage of time from birth to death. These rites include how people celebrate birth and marriage, and how they grieve death. Where a Christian world-view dominates, people practice these rites with their local congregations. Protestant Christians tend to celebrate birth (baptism or dedication), adulthood (profession of faith, confirmation, or baptism), marriage, and death in their congregation's sacred space or sanctuary with the assistance of pastors, who guide participants through prescribed liturgies. Roman Catholics practice seven sacraments that mark the passage of a person from birth to death. The first three—Baptism, Confirmation, and the Lord's Supper, commonly referred to as the "Sacraments of Initiation"—not only mark significant moments in life, but provide grace for life. The sacraments of Confession, Marriage, and Holy Orders mark time for some, but not all, Christians. The sacrament of the Anointing of the Sick, commonly referred to as Last Rites, is administered to the dying as well as to those hoping for the recovery of both physical health and for spiritual strength while enduring sickness.

For Christ-followers, the relationship between worship and culture represents an ever-present challenge. On one hand, we affirm the teaching of the apostle Paul, who taught us we are "fellow citizens with God's people" (Eph 2:19) and members of another kingdom. So, like Jesus, we are in the world but not of it (John 17:14). On the other hand, the world has a mind of its own, ever seeking to form us according to its values (1 John 2:15–18). Consequently, Jesus prays to God the Father for our protection (John 17:14–16) and the apostle Paul encourages vigilance by describing our life in this world as a war (Eph 6:10–20). When it comes to discipleship, we hope to follow Christ in this world while not being shaped by the values of this world. We desire to follow Christ in a particular context while being shaped by the Spirit and the Word (Jas 1:27, Rom 12:1–2).

When it comes to worship, we hope for the same. Towards that end, we adapt our worship to the community and culture of the worshipers. There are countless variations of this process for every corporate worship experience reflects, to one degree or another, its culture. Those who walk or ride a horse to worship outside a small home in the mountains of Honduras speak Spanish, worship in every day clothes, play acoustic guitars (since they are without electricity), and learn songs by repetition (since most do not read). Those who drive their cars to worship in a middle-to-upper income suburb in the United States dress upscale, speak English, employ electric technology, read bulletins, and sit in a "sacred" space called a "sanctuary."

While we readily acknowledge that worship is in the world, we also realize that worship is not of the world. We prefer that our worship not implicitly or explicitly affirm the values of this world. Instead, we hope our worship sustains the unique way of life taught and embodied by Jesus Christ, our beloved. As Stanley Hauerwas notes, the "primary social task of the church is to be itself."[5] So when we gather for worship as disciples of Jesus, we embrace another way of speaking, of building relationships, and of eating. Consequently, through our worship we reflect our new reality found in Christ. We also let the world know that there is "another language and another way of viewing and understanding reality that they should want to learn."[6]

---

5. Hauerwas, *Community of Character*, 10.
6. Brimlow, "Solomon's Porch," 110.

Worship, then, is in the world, but not of it. As Lukas Vischer writes, we seek to balance the "particularization" of the culture with the "universality" of the Gospel. Occasionally, we fall to one side or the other. At times we allow a particular aspect of culture to so shape our worship that it is no longer distinctively Christian. At other times we embrace a particular ritual that is so disconnected from life that it sounds like something from another planet. Our goal is somewhere in between. We pray for "authentic" worship, worship that is both faithful to God's revelation and to the situation in which we live.[7]

That kind of worship doesn't come easily. It calls for hard work and deep prayer. It requires "theologically informed cultural criticism of our environmental context;" it calls for a holy suspicion that culture accompanies every innovation, in one way or another.[8] It entails discernment. But when, by God's grace, we find the sweet spot of authenticity, our worship will exhibit both continuity and discontinuity with the culture. More importantly, when we find that spot, we will not need to "apologize for ways in which our worship differs from the broader culture;" nor will we feel pressured "to change worship simply because accommodation is easier than resistance to those pressures."[9] We will enjoy worship as a "radically countercultural and culture–transforming community" which calls "people into a new world . . . that includes new ways of worshiping, singing, and seeing all of life."[10]

Talking about authentic worship that is in the world but not of it sounds good, but requires diligence. Thankfully there is help, not only from the Holy Spirit who pours out his grace upon us, but from those who have come before us. One source of help is the aforementioned *Nairobi Statement of Worship and Culture: Contemporary Challenges and Opportunities*. After affirming that "worship is the heart and pulse of the Christian Church," and that, "Christian worship is always celebrated in a given local cultural setting." The *Nairobi Statement* describes four specific ways in which "Christian worship relates dynamically to culture." First, some elements of worship are *transcultural*. We find them wherever we find Christians in worship. Second, some elements of worship, like language or technology, are *contextual*. They represent specific aspects

---

7. Vischer, *Christian Worship in Reformed Churches*, 282.
8. Witvliet, *Worship Seeking Understanding*, 116.
9. *Authentic Worship in a Changing Culture*, 61.
10. Ibid.

of a particular community. Third, some elements of worship, such as reconciliation and hospitality, are *counter-cultural*. They "challenge what is contrary to the Gospel in a given culture." Fourth, some elements, like art, are cross-cultural, "making possible sharing between different local cultures."

The Nairobi Statement concludes with a challenge to undertake more efforts related to the transcultural, contextual, counter-cultural, and cross-cultural nature of Christian worship. That challenge includes, but is not limited to, a "call on all churches to give serious attention to exploring the local or contextual elements of liturgy, language, posture and gesture, hymnody and other music and musical instruments, and art and architecture for Christian worship—so that their worship may be more truly rooted in the local culture." Affirming that call, let's explore five contextual elements wherein we may experience tension between worship and culture. In this chapter, I will explore language, space, aesthetics (other than music), and technology. In the next, the contextual element of music.

Language

One of the lasting contributions of the Protestant Reformers was their insistence that worship be offered in the vernacular of a given people. Interestingly, Paul Wegner discovered that those people groups which did not receive the Scriptures in their own tongue—such as the early Berber Christians in North Africa—did not long persist in their Christianity.[11] Consequently, in this day and age, language represents the most prominent application of the "in, but not of" principle. In order to respond to our Triune God's invitation to worship him, we employ a human language (unless the Holy Spirit gifts us with a supernatural tongue). While worshiping the Lord in private, we may default to our mother tongue or "heart language." This is the language by which "we first learned to express love, joy, sorrow, and need." Our "heart language" is "rich in nuance, humor, gesture and inflection. It's the words you naturally dream in, the genres and image you use to change minds."[12] But when we gather with other Christians for worship, unless we are going for a Tower of

---

11. Wegner, *The Journey from Texts to Translations*.
12. Huyser-Honig, "Ethnodoxology."

Babel vibe, we must decide what language to employ. Let's call it a "liturgical language," so as to distinguish it from a "heart language."

While an exclusive decision, the selection of a liturgical language is necessary for any congregation that desires to worship the Lord with one heart and mind. This decision comes easy for most gatherings of Christians, since many of our communities, neighborhoods, and congregations form around shared languages. In some contexts, however, the selection of a liturgical language has the potential to provoke tremendous passion. Immigrant congregations, for example, inevitably struggle mightily with this issue. Typically such a congregation forms around the language of the immigrants. That decision is a good one. It allows immigrants to worship with their "heart language" and, thereby, fully express their love and devotion for the Lord.[13] It goes unchallenged until the children of immigrants acclimate to their new surroundings and learn the language of their new neighborhoods. These bilingual children can still worship with the language of their parents, but can also worship in their newly discovered second language. Yet, for the sake of peace and unity, as well as a spirit of appreciation for their heritage, they continue to worship with their "mother language," the language of their home. Tensions rise, however, with the next generation—the grandchildren of the immigrants. They have fully adapted to the new community and have no memories of the "old country." They are less likely to be bilingual, and often prefer to worship in their "heart language," which is usually the language of their classmates. Now the immigrant congregation must revisit its decision about its liturgical tongue or watch the newest generation gradually drift away from the fellowship. In time, the first generation immigrants, moved by love for Christ and his church, will agree to adopt the heart language of their grandchildren as their liturgical language. In the end, then, the first generation will be part of a congregation whose cultural trappings may be similar to the "old country," but whose liturgical language is foreign. This will frustrate them when called to worship. Discontinuity between heart language and liturgical language hinders worshipers struggling verbally to convey the thoughts and feelings of their hearts with accuracy. Yet, evidence of the growth of the local church and the spiritual development of another generation of disciples will help minimize their frustrations. Plus, when they worship in the quietness

---

13. Ibid.

of their homes—read the Scriptures, listen to sacred music, and offer prayers—they will revert to their "heart language."

I am reminded of a story told by my friend Dean. He was one of several sons of a Dutch immigrant. Most of this man's sons fought in World War II. Dean, one of the youngest children in the family, remembers how his father would pray for each son before he left home for service in the military. While the family gathered around the table for a meal, his father would seek the Lord's blessing on his departing son. Dean looks back at those occasions remembering that his dad would start his prayer in English but, without realizing it, start praying in Dutch. And why wouldn't he do so? Dutch was the language by which he "first learned to express love, joy, sorrow, and need."[14] It was the language in which he chose to lift up the burdens of his heart to the Lord.

The contextual element of language raises more issues than the adoption of a liturgical language. Another important decision awaits a congregation: will it pepper its worship with biblical and theological language? Or will it limit its vocabulary to that of the world? Those two options form two poles within which congregations typically worship. On one hand, we don't leave the vocabulary of the world when we gather with Christians for worship. While talking with one another and praying to the Lord, we employ human language, the whole kit and caboodle, including its unique phrases and idioms. On the other hand, as Christians we have inherited a dictionary of words which convey the truths of God's Word and the nature of our spiritual experiences. As a result, with but a few words we may articulate a specific set of beliefs to fellow Christians about subjects like the Trinity, incarnation, sanctification, the inspiration of Scripture, the priesthood of all believers, and maybe even the rapture.

We expect, then, the language of worship to differ from the language of the neighborhood. But how much difference should we expect to find? Those advocating a seamless transition from the street to the sanctuary prefer as little difference as possible. Those accenting the pilgrim character of a separated people who are citizens of heaven promote as much difference as possible. Most congregations appear to wind up somewhere between the two. But, while undocumented, I think it safe to assert that the liturgical language of most American Protestant Christians is more generic than biblical or theological. Spurred, perhaps, by a noble and appropriate desire to be "seeker-sensitive," many congregations minimize

---

14. Ibid.

the use of biblical and doctrinal language. Robert Brimlow is one of several scholars challenging that practice:

> The problem that the church ought to be confronting when faced with the Lord's charge to us to witness to the nations is not that of finding a way to translate the gospel so that pagans can understand it in their idiom. That is to fall prey to and transform the gospel into the values of the world when what we should be doing is transforming the world into the Kingdom of God. Rather, our problem as church is to find a way to let the world know that there is another language and another way of viewing and understanding reality that they should want to learn.[15]

Those words by Brimlow challenged me when I first heard them. For years, I leaned to the seeker-sensitive side of the liturgical-tongue pendulum. I even took pride in being a garbage truck driver turned preacher who spoke the language of the masses, bad grammar and all. However, in more recent years I have had a change of mind. The turning point came through conversations with my high-school-dropout father about his multiple heart surgeries. He talked with me as if he were a heart surgeon. I still marvel at my father's grasp of his medical condition and medical terminology. It allowed him to easily discuss each of his twelve pharmaceutical prescriptions. Then, when he gathered with friends who, like him, needed compartmentalized plastic boxes to keep their pills straight, his comprehension of medical terms allowed him to discuss his medical condition in great detail. But here is the irony: after over seventy years in the church, my father could only engage in elementary biblical and theological dialogue.

Some might say, "So what?" But let's ask, "Why is it that my father regularly employed medical terminology but seldom uttered doctrinal or theological words?" In retrospect, I wonder if I contributed to that reality. I have identified four choices I made that shaped conversations with my father (as well as with my congregants). First, I succumbed to intellectual elitism. I assumed that my father and people like him couldn't comprehend the deep truths of Scripture. Now I am quite sure he could have just as easily learned to describe his regeneration by the Holy Spirit and justification by faith as he described his multiple surgeries.

Second, I got sucked into the pervasive trap of substituting psychological language (words that describe feelings) for biblical language

---

15. Brimlow, "Solomon's Porch," 109–10.

(words that describe truth). Of course, this is not an either-or decision. We may and should use both. We may say, "I feel like a new person since deciding to follow Jesus Christ," and we may say, "I have been born again." We may say, "I feel like a huge burden has been lifted," and we may say, "I have been reconciled with God." The challenge for us is not to choose one or the other, but to use one without eliminating the other. Personally, I failed to realize that, while "psychotherapeutic language has helped many people, Christians included, it should be the church's second language; (it should) not (replace) the first language of theology."[16]

Third, I failed to recognize that the church is, as those outside it expect it to be, a counter-cultural community with a distinctive way of talking. As Rodney Clapp notes, "God is at work, of course, in all of reality, not merely in our fleeting hours of public worship. But humanity is a blinded race, and in worship we have a chance to look on the world as it truly is—the beloved and redeemed creation of God the Father, Son and Holy Spirit."[17]

Finally, I failed to recognize that by abandoning the distinctive language of Christianity, I helped move the church off of its moorings, thereby letting it float aimlessly into the culture as just another social institution indistinguishable from others. In the end, a generic church doesn't look a whole lot different than any number of social or human welfare organizations.

These days I encourage Christians to remember that, as a covenanted community of believers, we inherit a dictionary filled with words which help us talk to one another about the truths of this world and of the Gospel. Words like "regeneration" or "Trinity" summarize great experiential and Biblical truths. They help us understand what our beloved Triune God has been about in the world, in the church, and in our lives. They help us articulate real answers to real questions by real people. They help us communicate the way, the truth, and the life to one another and the world. Most importantly, they inform, even prompt, our loving worship of the Triune God.

---

16. Clapp, *A Peculiar People*, 105.
17. Ibid., 112.

Space

Years ago, while listening to the radio, the broadcaster reached over the air waves and hit me in the gut. His words went something like this: "Your wife should always drive a nicer car than you." He followed that bold statement with this question: "What kind of husband would drive a better car than his wife?" Those words hit me hard. At that time in my life, my car was newer and nicer than the one my wife drove around. But that is no longer the case. Why? As any husband knows, love shapes space. It even shapes the cars sitting in the garage. No surprise, then, that our love for God and neighbor shapes the space in which we gather for worship.

Corporate worship requires several different types of space. First, there is the space where we gather, the size of which will be determined by the number of people gathering for worship. Then, there is the space to move around: space to stand and sit, space to dance and kneel, space to huddle with others, space to come forward for prayer, and space to leave for the bathroom. Third, there is the space for musicians who prompt our worship. For some congregations, this means a choir loft, for others, an orchestra pit. Fourth, the gathering space includes an area for the transcultural practices of baptism and the Lord's Supper, though the group may leave one space for another and accomplish both. Fifth, the gathering space includes a place for the preacher or teacher; in this space we find some kind of lectern or pulpit. Finally, the place where Christians gather includes support space, such as handicapped-accessible entries, bathrooms, coat rooms, sound booths, closets, and the like.

How does our Beloved shape the space where we gather for worship each week? That question leads to many others, including this one: Does our Triune God prefer we worship in sacred (set apart) space or in common space? If we limit our search to the Old Testament for an answer to that question, the answer would be clear. God makes plain his preference for sacred space. But things get muddy when we move to the New Testament. There we find Christians gathering in homes.[18] Plus, we hear God's broken but blessed people described as the temple of the Lord. What are we to make of this?

Before we answer that question let's acknowledge that many Christians do not grapple with the issue of sacred or common space. Many Christians live in countries with governments hostile to the faith. Paul Marshall, in *Their Blood Cries Out*, calculates that 200 million Christians

---

18. Meeks, *The First Urban Christians*, 75–77.

worldwide live in daily fear of being arrested for their faith, and in more than sixty countries worldwide Christians suffer abuse, imprisonment, torture, and execution on account of their faith.[19] These brothers and sisters in Christ don't have the luxury of entertaining conversations about sacred or common space. Without resources or freedom to design and build sacred space for public worship, they worship wherever the exigencies of life allow. American Christians, however, enjoy religious freedom and are among the wealthiest people in the world. American congregations don't make decisions between purchasing sacred space and daily bread. As a people blessed with significant financial resources, we (should) ask questions like "How shall we disburse God's money?" or, "How does love for God shape our expenditures?"

Some answer those questions in ways that affirm the utilization of common space for worship. They believe it best to prioritize their financial resources for ministry, mission and mercy, instead of for brick and mortar. They choose to worship in gymnasiums or multi-purpose rooms rather than in sacred space. That particular approach has its share of adherents. Most who share this perspective also share the assumption that resources are limited and, hence, the decision before them is either-or: either sacred space or ministry, mission and mercy. Therein lies the deficiency in the argument. God's resources are not limited to what we can touch and see. They are not scarce. He is the creator of the universe and owns the cattle on a thousand hills (Ps 50:10). So, the decision facing American Christians is most often not between sacred space or ministry, mission and mercy. It is more often than not between sacred space and common space. The decision between the two is reached as we reflect on how we shall respond to the love of our Beloved in our particular context.

While Christians may gather for worship in any space, many congregations have chosen to worship in space consecrated for worship. In so doing, they follow in a train of countless congregations who believe that God's love for us calls forth the best we can offer in love to our Beloved. They also implicitly or explicitly acknowledge that space can "elevate the human spirit," "speak of what cannot be fully understood," and remind us of a "holiness beyond words."[20]

Coincidentally, culture-watchers inform us that, in our post-Christian context, some people long for traditional sacred space. (Hence the

---

19. Marshall, *Their Blood Cries Out*, 8.
20. Rice and Huffstutler, *Reformed Worship*, 131.

popularity of Taize.) Nathan Bierma notes a trend away from warehouse looking buildings to a more antiquated look.[21] This preference represents Robert Webber's "ancient–future" dictum that the old is now new.[22] Bierma also notes a LifeWay survey commissioned by Cornerstone Knowledge.[23] LifeWay showed over 1,600 unchurched adults four pictures of church buildings, ranging from utilitarian, mall-like to ornate Gothic. Here's what the survey revealed: "By a nearly 2-to-1 ratio over any other option, unchurched Americans prefer churches that look more like a medieval cathedral than what most think of as a more contemporary church building."

The congregation that opts for sacred space will give special attention to the broader subject of architecture and the narrower subject of furnishings. Authors Donald Bruggink and Carl Droppers begin their unparalleled work, *Christ and Architecture*, with these words:

> Architecture for churches is a matter of gospel. A church that is interested in proclaiming the gospel must also be interested in architecture, for year after year the architecture of the church proclaims a message that either augments the preached Word or conflicts with it.[24]

Bruggink and Droppers validate their thesis with a reference to God's detailed concern over the construction of the tabernacle and the temple, and with an illustration from the sixteenth-century Reformation:

> The inherited Roman Catholic churches were not changed because of aesthetic inclinations on the part of the Reformed clergy, or because of a new stylistic fad. They were changed because the gospel was so important that the Reformers could not allow the churches to remain as they were. The Reformers were acutely conscious of the power of architecture and the constant message that it held for the people.[25]

In recent years, the thesis of Bruggink and Croppers has been affirmed by a growing number of Evangelical congregations, planted in large urban settings, purchasing and restoring facilities that were first built by Roman Catholics.

21. Bierma, "Keeping Holy Ground Holy."
22. See, for example, Webber, *Ancient-Future Faith*.
23. Perry, "LifeWay Research."
24. Bruggink and Droppers, *Christ and Architecture*, 1.
25. Ibid., 2.

Hopefully, each congregation wrestles with the implications of its theology for its space. This is just another way in which our Beloved shapes the space of worshipers. In his book *Worship Wars*, Thomas Long writes:

> A good worship space is not merely the result of decor; it is also the product of mature theological reflection about the nature of worship. Form follows function, and well-planned sanctuaries communicate by their very design the kind of worship that takes place within.[26]

Congregations whose liturgies include "altar calls" will be designed with balconies spilling into the main floor. Congregations which believe that the preaching of the Word is the center piece of the liturgy will place the pulpit front and center, with pews facing the pulpit. Congregations which believe that people enter the church through baptism may place their baptismal at the entrance of the sanctuary. Congregations who highlight congregational singing may choose not to carpet the pews and floors and, thereby, optimize the acoustic qualities of their gathering spaces.

Not all of our current sacred space makes theological sense. The Scriptures call Christians to kneel before the Lord our Maker (Ps 95:6), but few Protestant sanctuaries have kneelers. It seems the sixteenth-century Reformers removed them from the sanctuary thinking them essentially "Roman." A long sanctuary with two sections of twenty pews separated by a center aisle is not as conducive to the manifold purposes of our gathering as a shorter and wider fan-shaped sanctuary with four sections of ten pews each. Most Lord's Supper tables barely resemble the dinner tables in our homes. When placed against a wall, the Lord's Supper table looks more like an altar upon which one makes a sacrifice (or a place for a large floral arrangement leftover from someone's funeral) than the table upon which Christ shared the Passover feast with the apostles. Finally, most sanctuary crosses are too pretty and fail to convey accurately its offensive nature. They are neither old or rugged.

Perhaps the most difficult issue facing many congregations is inherited space that hinders rather than enhances the loving worship of a congregation. Many sanctuaries, for example, limit accessibility to the able-bodied, provide minimal space for instrumentalists, have poor sight lines and lighting, and most importantly, fail to reflect the beauty and grandeur of God. If the Lord provides the resources, congregations with

26. Long, *Beyond the Worship War*, 67.

such restrictions may want to consider modifying their sacred spaces or constructing new spaces. Congregants, however, tend to cherish their inherited spaces, an understandable emotion. In those same spaces they have shared countless memories of God's grace. It's holy ground to them. Consequently, they resist attempts for change or modification, even those motivated by love. Take, as one example, efforts to make a campus or facility accessible to all. Such an initiative seems like a no-brainer for a congregation desiring to reflect the hospitality of the Lord. Yet, some congregations resist such moves, even when funds are readily accessible. Then and there we witness a gap between worship and love. Then and there love for God and neighbor does not shape our decisions about space. Then and there our space becomes an idol, though few recognize it as such.

Aesthetics (other than music)

God has created a world characterized by a beauty that exerts power on people. In Genesis 2:9 we read that "the Lord God made all kinds of trees to grow out of the ground—trees that were pleasing to the eye and good for food." In Genesis 3:6 we read that the "woman saw that the fruit of the tree was good for food and pleasing to the eye." We may conclude with William Dyrness that, "The world seems to be shaped in such a way that it welcomes our appreciation of its beauty."[27] Who would argue that God has created a beautiful world and that beauty is powerful? Dyrness writes:

> Something of the loving goodness of God shines through our experience of beauty. This is why we are inevitably moved to put ourselves in the way of such experiences. We deeply long not only for such beauty but, Christians believe, for relationship with the personal presence lying beneath such beauty. As a result, the experience of great beauty often moves unbelievers to seek God, just as it often moves believers to praise, even to sing or dance.[28]

Conversations about beauty bring us to the subject of aesthetics, a word which speaks to a culture's sense of the beautiful or love of beauty. The study of aesthetics grapples with a particular culture's view and perception of beauty. It deals with the nature and expression of beauty, human

27. Dyrness, *Visual Faith*, 141.
28. Ibid., 142.

responses to beauty, and how communities determine what is beautiful. As such, aesthetics speak more to the emotive than cognitive side of life. Typically, we first acknowledge beauty before analyzing. We first see something and perceive it as beautiful, then we seek to understand the details of its construction. As an adjective, the word "aesthetically" refers to that which reflects a love of beauty. As an academic discipline, the study of aesthetics leads to participation in what have been called "Fine Arts" or "Visual Arts" or "Performing Arts." These arts include, but are not limited to, music, architecture, painting, sculpture, poetry, drama, photography, and dancing.

The question before us concerns the dynamic interplay between love and worship and beauty. We, who have been loved by God our Father, redeemed by God the Son, and indwelt by God the Spirit, long to respond with loving worship of our beautiful Triune God. Love itself is beautiful and requires no adornment, but this does not hinder lovers from longing to worship the beloved with that which is beautiful. Love needs no explanation for this desire but may find it within the image of God which characterizes each lover. As human beings created in the image of God, we have been gifted, to one degree or another, and in one area or another, to create that which is beautiful. The dominant impulse for that work is our love for beauty. At times we may submit to lesser motives, such as financial gain or emotional manipulation, but the best motive remains love. Like God, we enjoy creating that which is good. Consequently, we hope and pray that love will bring that which is beautiful to the altar of worship.

Since the gifts of the Holy Spirit differ with each Christian, these loving and beautiful acts of worship come in many varieties. They come in many forms for the resources of one Christian differ from those of another. They come in many degrees, for the Holy Spirit, "the source of genuine artistic creativity," has poured out special creative gifts on some of his children.[29] Some among us lovingly respond to God's beauty and grace in ways that arrest our attentions, move our emotions, and still our spirits. Visual artists, for example, create beautiful artifacts. Some of them find a home in a downtown gallery or an emerging gallery on the campus of a congregation. Others may even find their way into the sanctuary where their beauty will not only stand as a congregation's act of loving worship, but also enrich the worship of those gathered.

---

29. Calvin, *Institutes of the Christian Religion* II.2.15–16.

Artists who have been gifted by God to create that which is beautiful are scattered throughout the world. Many of them also have a place in the body of Christ. Each week they gather with other Christians for corporate worship of our Triune God. Wired as they are, the best way they know how to express their love for God is through the arts. The question for local congregations, then, is whether or not they will empower artists to share their gift so that together they can lovingly worship the Lord through the arts.

Over the years, the answer to that question has been a resounding "No!" The entire Christian Church hasn't answered in that fashion. Orthodox Christians and Roman Catholics have employed the arts in worship, but, by and large, the Protestant Church has not done so. That resistance finds roots in the sixteenth-century Protestant Reformation. The Reformers implemented a dramatic reform of corporate worship, one that included the stripping of the sanctuary of everything but the pulpit, Bible, Lord's Supper table, and baptismal. As a result, Protestants have a history of violent iconoclasm and a long tradition of minimizing the role of the arts in worship. The Heidelberg Catechism, a sixteen-century tutorial for Reformed Christians, has contributed to that tradition. Here is a sequence of questions and answers from its "Lord's Day 35":

- Question 96: What is God's will for us in the second commandment?
- Answer: That we in no way make any image of God nor worship him in any other way than he has commanded in his Word.
- Question 97: May we then not make any image at all?
- Answer: God cannot and may not be visibly portrayed in any way. Although creatures may be portrayed, yet God forbids making or having such images if one's intention is to worship them or to serve God through them.
- Question 98: But may not images be permitted in the churches as teaching aids for the unlearned?
- Answer: No, we shouldn't try to be wiser than God. He wants his people instructed by the living preaching of his Word—not by idols that cannot even talk.

Perhaps it is time to acknowledge, explicitly rather than implicitly, that the Protestant Reformers, influenced by their own culture and context, may have over-reacted. In the spirit of the "reformed, but always reforming" Protestant Reformers, maybe it is time to cast a new vision for the inclusion of art in worship. If we allow that possibility, we have permission to craft a new confession by Christians who take seriously the potential for art to help (or hinder) the corporate worship of the faithful. Such a document would open the door for congregations to call and empower gifted artists to employ their God-given gifts in a way that enriches the ministry of the gathered community. Some of their work may even find its way into the sanctuary, because of the "depth of its human expression or because of the sense of transcendence that its beauty generates."[30]

If a new confession sounds too daunting, perhaps congregations can work together to form guidelines for the relationship between art and loving worship by the local church. Through such a document, local congregations would be able to affirm both artists and the function of art in their ministries while also articulating guidelines which can be applied by knowledgeable advisors—Christians who know both art and the congregation's doctrinal statements. Without such guidelines, gathering spaces and sanctuaries may take on the appearance of craft show in a local gymnasium. There will be a little bit of this and a little bit of that, but no common thread connecting one to the other. While politically difficult, congregations that succeed in this area will find ways to say "no" to certain aspects and forms of art while joyously affirming art as a gift from God.[31] They will do so because artistry requires discernment, just like the exercise of other gifts.

The congregation that affirms artists and art faces a few challenges. First, the congregation that commits to the arts will have to back up that decision with financial resources. Individuals who have been called and gifted by God to serve Christ and the world as artists need not be "starving artists" for the sake of the Gospel. The church need not expect artists to share their gifts with the church free of charge. Instead, the church may choose to support and empower brothers and sisters who have been gifted to create beautiful artifacts. Towards that end, a commitment to art must be accompanied by a budget which allows for the purchasing of art and commissioning of artists.

The second challenge speaks to power of art to tempt the deficiencies of human nature. We are sinning saints, broken vessels, and imperfect disciples. Like Paul, we wrestle constantly with our desires and behaviors.

---

30. Brown, *Good Taste, Bad Taste, and Christian Taste*, 55.
31. See, for example, the art of Robert Mapplethorpe or Vito Acconci.

So, in the area of the arts, we must be on guard that our love for beauty doesn't turn into a love of self, that our appreciation for the visible doesn't reflect a lack of faith in that which is invisible, and that our admiration for that which is beautiful doesn't hinder worship of the one who is beautiful. In other words, we must keep art in its place. John De Gruchy writes,

> Art enhances faith, but is not a replacement for faith. Art provides a vehicle for the Spirit, but is not the power of the Spirit . . . Great art speaks to the soul . . . (It) helps us perceive reality in a new way, and by so doing, it opens up possibilities of transformation.[32]

Third, there is the danger, as de Gruchy notes, of ecclesiastical art degenerating, on the one hand, into an uncritical ecclesial kitsch or, on the other hand, conforming to the dictates of "high culture." In such cases, art loses its "theological integrity and coherence."[33] This challenge cannot be overestimated for it may be a congregation's primary reason for minimizing the role of art in worship. Congregational leaders struggle with affirming art because they envision a future when they may have to inform a sincere Christian that his or her aesthetic contribution to the community is not up to their standards. They foresee a time when they will be called upon to pass judgment in an area where they have little experience or expertise. That is a legitimate concern that must be dealt with on a case-by-case basis. There will be times when we blur the distinction between that which is beautiful and that which is not. Such is the nature of aesthetics. But that need not paralyze a congregation and hinder it from affirming the place of art among a people who simply want to love their beloved through worship.

Technology

When I reflect on the relationship between love and technology I remember my very first Skype conversation. I was sitting in my home in Illinois and connected with my son serving in the Armed Forces in Afghanistan. While thousands of miles apart, we communicated face to face. It was as if we were in the same room. That use of technology was motived by love. But what if my other son texted me from his bedroom while I sat in the family room of the same house? Would you describe that use of

32. de Gruchy, "Holy Beauty," 21–22.
33. Ibid., 16.

technology as motivated by love or perhaps, by laziness? Those two illustrations illustrate this truth: the use of technology may be prompted by love or by less noble motives.

The question before us is, "How do we lovingly worship God through technology?" Ironically, the beginning place for developing an answer to that question is a place without technology—the Garden of Eden. In Genesis 1:26 we read these words of God, "Let us make man in our image, in our likeness, and let them rule over the fish of the sea and the birds of the air, over the livestock, over all the earth, and over all the creatures that move along the ground." Al Wolters is one among many who refer to that verse as the cultural or creation mandate. Commenting on its significance, he writes,

> The creation mandate provides a sort of climax to the six days of creation. The stage with all its rich variety of props has been set by the stage director, the actors are introduced, and as the curtain rises and the stage director moves backstage, they are given their opening cure. The drama of human history is about to begin, and the first and foundational Word of God to his children is the command to "fill and subdue."[34]

When we move to the second chapter of Genesis, we find God creating Adam from the earth and placing "him in the Garden of Eden to work it and take care of it" (Gen 2:15). The Lord, then, creates Eve as Adam's companion and co-worker. Together, as co-equals, Adam and Eve "represent the beginnings of societal life; their task of tending the garden, the primary task of agriculture, represents the beginnings of cultural life."[35]

Like Adam and Eve, we care for God's creation. We "participate in the ongoing creational work of God, to be God's helper in executing to the end the blueprint for his masterpiece." We do so with optimism, relishing the opportunity to bring "to fruition the possibilities of development implicit in the work of God's hands." We recognize that the created order includes the potential for the development of great marvel, as well as "positive possibilities for service to God in such areas as politics and the film arts, computer technology and business administration, developmental economics and skydiving."[36]

---

34. Wolters, *Creation Regained*, 37–38.
35. Ibid.
36. Ibid.

The creation mandate provides the foundation upon which we develop an answer to the question of how to lovingly worship God through technology. Perhaps no one has built on that foundation better than Quentin Schultze, Professor of Communication Arts and Science at Calvin College in Grand Rapids, Michigan. In his book *High Tech Worship*, Schultze offers several tools for contemporary Christians seeking to experience a loving relationship between technology and worship. First, he provides a useful description of technology.[37] In his estimation, technology includes: the physical devices or tools that we use to develop God's creation, the meanings that we attach to these devices, and the ways that we use them. We may flesh out Schultze's threefold description through application. One technology at the heart of the sixteenth-century Reformation was the printing press (a tool), which led to the mass production of the Bible (its use), so that Christians could read the Bible in their native tongue (its value). One of the more popular technologies in modern worship, to cite another example, is an amplification system, a tool that magnifies the preacher's voice (its use) so that Christians can hear the sermon (its value).

Second, Schultze reminds us that, "Worship always relies on human skills and techniques, if not particular technologies." Looking over the history of the Church, we discover that, motivated by love, "worshipers have long fashioned raw materials into such worship artifacts as chalices, stained glass, candles, incense, and crosses."[38] The questions we face today, therefore, are not new. God's children perpetually wrestle with discerning the relationship between worship and technology. Sometimes our wrestling leads to marvelous results, such as the use of a printing press or an amplification system. Sometimes we error and create golden calves or ineffective power point slides.

Third, and most important for this conversation, Schultze asserts that "communication technologies are not neutral tools that merely carry intended messages." Technologies convey messages.[39] When they work as designed, they convey a message of "power, efficiency, and control;" they leave us with the impression that life is neatly packaged and slick. When they don't work as designed, they connote messages more consistent with

---

37. Schultze, *High-Tech Worship*, 43.
38. Ibid., 17.
39. Borgmann, *Power Failure*.

our reality: they remind us that both life and love are not always efficient or predictable or under our control.

Years ago, a woman who had experienced the wonderful grace of Jesus, illustrated as much. To the dismay of others, and without regard for efficiency or slickness, she poured an alabaster box full of perfume over the head of Jesus (Matt 26:6–12). This was her loving act of worship. Similarly, our worship is not always efficient. Instead, as Marva Dawn notes, it is a "royal waste of time" and complicates love.[40] From time to time, then, worship bucks up against technology and refuses to be confined to that which has been prescribed. Nothing—not even the time on the clock or the lack of electrical power—can hold back the worship of one overwhelmed by God's grace.

In his work, *Power Failure: Christianity in the Culture of Technology*, Albert Borgmann adds another consideration to this discussion of the relationship between technology and loving worship. He observes that technology is a device that makes life easier; it makes something available to us in a comfortable manner.[41] In today's day and age, we accomplish many tasks without ever leaving our homes. Scholars complete a significant percentage of their research without stepping into a library. Shoppers may purchase gifts, groceries, and garments without going to a mall. Christians listen to sermons and worship the Lord before getting out of their pajamas. Overseas missionaries remain in their fields of service while streaming a video to their congregations at home.

Surely all would agree that technology makes life easier and, for that reason, it doesn't always suggest love. My wife could have told you that! For some reason, ordering a gift online doesn't seem to cut it with her. She prefers that I exert time and energy by going to the mall and walking in and out of several stores. She likes when I manually purchase a gift and wrap it, when I take the extra effort to purchase and attach a card to it. She likes when I take all those steps before offering her a gift. It seems that, in her estimation, a gift purchased with effort expresses more love than a gift purchased with minimal effort. Perhaps her views have been influenced by David who refused to give the Lord that which cost him nothing (II Samuel 24:24). Hence, when asked if technology is a value-neutral tool, Borgmann forcefully responded:

---

40. Dawn, *A Royal "Waste" of Time*.
41. Borgmann, *Power Failure*.

No. It's an inducement, and it's so strong that for the most part people find themselves unable to refuse it. To proclaim it to be a neutral tool flies in the face of how people behave. Why do 90 percent of all families or households watch television after dinner? Is it because they decided that that's the best way to spend their time? No, something else must be going on. And what's going on is that the culture around us—including work that is draining, food that's easily available, and television shows made as attractive as some of the best minds in our country can make them encourages us to plop down in front of the TV and spend two hours there.[42]

Borgmann prompts us to ask questions. Is worship aided by more technology more or less loving than worship aided by less technology? How much technology is too much? When does technology hinder loving worship? When does it help worship and when does it get in the way? What level of slickness (excellence?) shall we seek in our corporate worship? There are no easy answers to those questions. Each one, plus many more, can only be answered—and must be answered—within the particular context where Scripture and technology meet and dance. In each community, the dance looks different.

Fourth, Schultze encourages us to view technology as a means to an end, not an end in itself. He encourages us to "begin with God's intrinsic designs for worship rather than with a mere human desire for technological efficiency and control—as if we could socially engineer perfect worship on our own without God."[43] On this matter we find two polls within which congregations find themselves. At one end, we have congregations who, week in and week out, use technology as a means to strengthen the worship of God's people. They understand worship as a corporate, unifying experience. They use sound to support, not overpower the singing of the congregation. They employ visuals which enhance worship and that do not distract attention away from the Triune God. At the other end, we have congregations who seem to be enthralled with technology. They use it just for the sake of using it, even though it may hinder, even distort the worship of God's people. Most congregations live between those two polls. With the help of the Spirit's gifts of wisdom and discernment, they seek to employ technology in such a way that it encourages loving

---

42. Wood, "Prime Time."
43. Schultze, *High-Tech Worship*, 23.

HOW THE BELOVED SHAPES THE CONTEXT OF WORSHIP

worship of our Triune God. In the presence of such splendor, technology must, out of necessity, withdraw to its subordinate status.[44]

Fifth, Schultze provides a balanced perspective about the use of technology in worship. He reminds that the use of technology is not either-or; it is "Yes, but."

> Yes, we will consider using it to service our neighbors as ourselves, but we will not be duped by inflated rhetoric about its inherent goodness or badness. Yes, new technologies are part of the unfolding of God's original creation, but we fallen human beings will never be able to use them to usher in heaven on earth. The yes is our faith in God to bless our imperfect use of technology; the but is our admission of foolishness and hubris—all sin.[45]

As Christians seeking both to lovingly worship God and fulfill the creation mandate, we resist the temptation to suppose that "any technological innovation has a one-sided effect." We realize, as Neil Postman writes that "every technology is both a burden and a blessing; not either-or, but this-and-that."[46] Consequently, we don't adopt technology, but adapt it to serve our specific purposes for congregation-specific, loving worship of our Triune God. This quote by Theodore Roszak on the counter-culturally impulse of Christianity, in general, and worship, in particular, aptly sums up our objective as Christians with regard to technology:

> The primary project of our counter culture: to proclaim a new heaven and a new earth so vast, so marvelous that the inordinate claims of technical expertise must of necessity withdraw in the presence of such splendor to a subordinated and marginal status in the lives of men.[47]

Conclusion

The Triune God we worship is creating "a chosen people, a royal priesthood, a holy nation." This mission will continue until the Lord determines

---

44. See Roszak, *The Making of a Counter Culture*, 240.
45. Schultze, *High-Tech Worship*, 43.
46. Postman, *Technopoly*, 4–5.
47. Roszak, *The Making of a Counter Culture*, 240.

it is completed. Until that day we will "declare the praises of him who called (us) out of darkness into his wonderful light" (1 Pet 2:9–10), and we will do so within a particular culture, one that shapes our worship. Consequently, our worship here on earth will always be culturally conditioned. The environment we superimpose on nature will include three essential ingredients: values which direct our lives, the patterns or predictable and typical ways that individuals within a community celebrate life together, and the institutions or traditional rites by which communities mark the passage of time from birth to death.

For Christ-followers, the relationship between worship and culture represents a vexing, perennial challenge. We hope to follow Christ in this world while not being shaped by the values of this world. We hope to follow Christ in a particular context while being shaped by the Spirit and the Word. When it comes to worship, we hope for the same. Toward that end, we adapt our worship to the community and culture of the worshipers. We balance the particularization of the culture with the universality of the Gospel. In the process, we discover that some elements of worship are transcultural, others counter-cultural, still others cross-cultural, and most contextual. In this chapter, we have looked at four contextual elements: language, space, aesthetics (other than music), and technology. Now it is time to look at music.

chapter 7

HOW THE BELOVED SHAPES THE MUSIC OF WORSHIP

Wherever we find people, we hear music. As ethnomusicologist Bruno Nettl notes, "All societies have something that sounds to us like music" and all "humans can identify music, though not necessarily understand it."[1] As early as Genesis 4:21, the Bible refers to musicians and two musical instruments: the lyre and flute. The topic of music brings us back to the field of aesthetics and the subject of fine art, a subject that is notoriously elusive. I begin with the simple affirmation that music is an art form by which artists create new pieces through unique combinations of tones, rhythms, instruments, and lyrics.

As an art form, music reflects three characteristics. First, like other art forms, music prizes beauty even while there is little agreement on how to measure that quality. Some narratives in the Bible, such as those which describe the construction of the temple in Jerusalem, reference possible aesthetic standards. But, what's beautiful to me may not be beautiful to you. When all is said and done, when it comes to music, one is left suggesting that we'll know beautiful music when we hear it. Therein rests the problem with measuring beauty. Second, music is "more distant from nature" than other art forms inasmuch as musicians don't handle material stuff.[2] They make melodies and harmonies; they don't shape clay or put paint to canvas. One wonders if this explains, in part, its prominence

1. Nettl, *Study of Ethnomusicology*, 25.
2. Ibid., 246.

in Judeo-Christian worship, a tradition which includes clear admonitions against the worship of "graven images" (Exodus 20). Third, and most important for this conversation, music, like other art forms, speaks primarily from and to the emotive side of humanity. Plus, as it speaks, it both expresses and induces emotion. In other words, while musicians communicate or express emotion through music, the music they communicate induces emotion from the listener. Like the provocative nature of prose, music appears to do so by conjuring up memories. When a particular song is connected in our memory to a particular context, such as to a person or event such as death, the playing of the song induces emotions.[3]

The emotive quality explains the dynamic relationship between music and love. Music may be the most prominent, pervasive, and powerful tool by which one person expresses love for another person or people or country or god. Lovers may utilize other art forms for that same purpose, such as painting, sculptures, and photography (the 1884 painting "Dante and Beatrice" by Henry Holiday comes to mind), but such art forms are not as accessible to lovers as music. Suffice it to say that, in this day and age, where you find love you will hear music—and both will be beautiful.

Since music and love enjoy a dynamic relationship, we are not surprised to discover that Christians have, for centuries, embraced music as a way to express love for the Lord. The end result has been a "dazzling variety of liturgical music." John Witvliet observes:

> For twenty centuries, Christians at worship have sung everything from contemplative Byzantine chants to exuberant Methodist frontier songs, from the trancelike music of Taize' refrains to the precise rhetoric of Watts and Wesley, from songs with the Dionysian ecstasy of African-American gospel anthems to those with the Apollonian reserve of a Presbyterian metrical psalm, from the serene beauty of a Palestrina motet to the rugged earthiness of an Appalachian folk tune, and from the enforced silence of Quaker corporate mysticism to the sustained exuberance of an African-American ring-shout sermon."[4]

Now, at the beginning of a new century, I wonder how God's love for us, his people, will shape the music we employ in worship. Shall we step off the great train of witnesses who have gone before us? Or shall we join them and seek, with all our heart, soul, mind, and strength, to offer deep,

---

3 For more on this subject, see Patzschke, "Empathy Towards the Performer."
4. Witvliet, "Beyond Style," 67.

passionate, authentic, and loving worship to the Lord through music? Shall we embrace the spiritual practice of singing, a practice which is also intrinsic to our personhood (which is why it stings so much when someone tells us we sing poorly)?[5]

In an attempt to answer those questions, I now describe a handful of factors that may be considered by lovers hoping to express love for their Beloved through music. These factors include the power of music, the function of music, the types of music, and the styles of music. But I begin by returning to the aforementioned subject of the prevalence of music.

The Prevalence of Music

Music plays an important role in our personal lives and permeates our weekly gatherings with other Christ-followers. In fact, I have yet to worship with a community of believers whose worship does not include music. Music is an assumed entailment to worship, even for pagans like Nebuchadnezzar (Dan 3:1–11). Surely it is safe to conclude that when God's people come together, songs fill their hearts and they sing.

The prevalence of music in worship doesn't surprise those familiar with the Scriptures, for from there it finds unquestioned support. Many passages readily come to mind, including Psalm 95: "Come, let us sing for joy to the Lord; let us shout aloud to the Rock of our salvation. Let us come before him with thanksgiving, and extol him with music and song. For the Lord is the great God, the great King above all gods" (Psalm 95:1–3). In Ephesians 5:17 we read, "speak to one another with psalms, hymns and Holy Spirit songs." In addition to scriptural mandates and prescriptions, we find countless examples in the Scriptures of God's people employing music as they worship their Triune God. During the exodus from Egypt, Miriam the prophetess took her tambourine and led the women in song and dance as they celebrated the Lord's triumph over the Egyptians (Exod 15:20–1). In Judges 5 we read the Song of Deborah," written by the prophetess and judge of the same name who led God's people to military victory. Saul once encountered a band of sanctuary prophets who prophesied accompanied by instruments (1 Sam 10:5). Isaiah composed songs, including one celebrating the Lord's deliverance of those who trust in him (Isa 26:1–6). People regarded Ezekiel as "one who

---

5. See Bass and Briehl, eds., *On Our Way*.

has a beautiful voice and plays well on an instrument" (33:32).[6] Finally, in one of the more remarkable passages, the Scriptures teach us that, while we offer our loving worship, our Triune God sings over us: "The Lord your God is in your midst, a mighty one who will save; he will rejoice over you with gladness; he will quiet you with his love; he will exult over you with loud singing" (Zeph 3:17 ESV).

Before leaving the theme of the prevalence of music in worship, I add that it cannot be entirely explained anthropologically. On one hand, the emotive quality of music suggests that the worship of any people to any god will include music, as in the aforementioned Nebuchadnezzar. On the other hand, music functions as a symbol and fruit of God's blessing or presence in our lives. In the Old Testament, it functions as a sign of national flourishing (Isa 38:20). Conversely, the judgment of God entails the cessation of music (Lam 5:14; Ezek 26:13). In the New Testament, as Gordon Fee notes, "Where the Spirit of God is, there is also singing. The early church was characterized by singing; so also in every generation where there is renewal by the Spirit a new hymnody breaks forth."[7] The correlation between the Holy Spirit and song may be affirmed because the Holy Spirit gives every good and perfect gift (Jas 1:17). The Spirit gifts some among us to create music, others among us to accompany our worship, and still others among us to inspire our worship. In this way, we, the people of God, are never without a song. Even in heaven, the redeemed of the Lord will sing a new song (Rev 14:1–4).

The Power of Music

One reason music saturates our lives is that music elevates, if not transforms experience. Music "does something to a person, something not done by anything else; nothing can be substituted for it."[8] Centuries ago the pastor-theologian John Calvin acknowledged that music has "a secret, almost incredible force to move our hearts in one way or another."[9] John Wesley once stated that music has "power to affect the hearers; to

---

6. Leonard, "Music and Worship in the Bible."

7. Fee, *Paul, the Spirit, and the People of God*, 159.

8. Nettl, *Study of Ethnomusicology*, 250.

9. From John Calvin's preface to his 1542 "Form of Prayers and Ecclesiastical Chants With the Manner of Administering the Sacraments and of Solemnizing Marriage According to Customs of the Ancient Church." A similar quote may be found in Calvin's "Forward to the Psalter," 94.

raise various passions in the human mind . . . to inspire love or hate, joy or sorrow, hope or fear, courage, fury, or despair . . . and to vary the passion just according to the variation of the music."[10]

My wife and I have both witnessed and experienced the power of music on many occasions, but one now comes to mind. We attended an outdoor concert featuring two of our favorite bands: *Chicago* and *Earth, Wind and Fire*. We were sitting on the lawn waiting for the concert to begin—but there was a delay. As we, with many in the audience, grew restless, the person handling the sound system took over. She started playing songs from television shows of the 60s and 70s, music from programs like *The Andy Griffith Show, Leave it To Beaver, Dick Van Dyke Show*, and the *Mary Tyler Moore Show*. An amazing thing happened. The crowd, which consisted mostly of people who grew up during the 60s and 70s, began to sing along, seemingly forgetting about the delay in the concert. The music had replaced our impatience with patience; it settled the crowd.

Similar experiences may be shared by countless Christians whose souls have been soothed and spirits elevated by music. While acknowledging the tremendous power of music, we best also acknowledge its coercive power. Music, like electricity, is a tremendous blessing, but when handled inappropriately, it can mess you up. Music has power to move, but also manipulate our hearts, as in the North Korean lullaby entitled "Shoot Americans." The power of music explains why the style of music in one place differs from the style of music in another. The music in a night club differs from the music in a dentist's office. The music at a sporting event differs from the music at funeral.

Without a doubt, music has the power to soften people up or harden their resolve, to break people down or lift people up. In short, music can be used in a manipulative manner to shape a particular show of emotion or action—and has been used in such a way, even in sanctuaries built in the name of Christ. May the Lord forgive us when we use music to manipulate people rather than as a tool by which we express love.

The Function of Music

Music serves many social functions in society. Alan P. Merriam lists as many as ten: "emotional expression, aesthetic enjoyment, entertainment, communication, symbolic representation, physical response, enforcing

10. "Thoughts on the Power of Music," in *John Wesley's Teachings*, III:470, sec 1.

conformity to social norms, validation of social institutions and religious rituals, contribution to the continuity and stability of culture, and contribution to the integration of society."[11] Personal experience confirms Merriam's list. During my lifetime, I have experienced each of those functions; perhaps you have, as well.

Merriam's list prompts follow-up questions. *"How does music function when we gather as God's people for worship?" "How does music function in my attempts to love my Beloved through worship?"* Remove the function of entertainment, and Merriam's list pretty well describes the variety of ways music functions when God's people gather. Music allows Christians to express themselves emotionally. Music, such as a choral anthem or solo, provides aesthetic enjoyment for the listener and concurrently points the listener to God. Music, especially the right combination of lyric and melody, communicates the deep truths of God's Word. Take, as an example, the great hymn of Charles Wesley "And Can It Be," and its melody written by Thomas Campbell. It begins:

> And can it be that I should gain
> an interest in the Savior's blood!
> Died he for me? who caused his pain!
> For me, who him to death pursued?
> Amazing love! How can it be
> that thou, my God, shouldst die for me?

In addition, congregational singing symbolically represents the congregation's unity in Christ and provides an opportunity for the worshiper to respond to God's grace. Finally, music also shapes our identity as a congregation by transmitting our shared faith (enforcing conformity), supporting our rituals (the Lord's Supper), contributing to the creation of a congregational culture, and by allowing even the newest of Christians to experience integration in the congregation.

While Christians may employ music for each of the functions listed by Merriam, my focus here is on the function of music in support of corporate worship. When we gather as a congregation, we may speak words of praise, perhaps through a unison reading of a Psalm or by a spontaneous "Hallelujah." We may accompany our spoken words with the clapping of hands (Ps 47:1), or with the lifting of our hands (Ps 63:4 and 1 Tim 2:8), or with dancing (Ps 149:3). We may offer silent prayers as our lips remain silent while our hearts burst forth in praise (Ps 4:7).

---

11. Merriam, *The Anthropology of Music*, 219.

HOW THE BELOVED SHAPES THE MUSIC OF WORSHIP

Finally, however, we must sing. Our love for the Beloved will not rest until we sing. As Karl Barth once wrote:

> The Christian community sings. It is not a choral society. Its singing is not a concert. But from inner, material necessity it sings. Singing is the highest form of human expression . . . The praise of God which finds its concrete culmination in the singing of the community is one of the indispensable basic forms of the ministry of the community.[12]

In a similar vein, Dietrich Bonhoeffer suggests that, "It is the voice of the church that is heard in singing together."[13]

The Types of Music

Over the centuries, Christians have employed several different types of songs as they worshiped their Beloved. The Apostle Paul indicates that the first-century Christians sang psalms, hymns, and Holy Spirit songs (Col 3:16). Since those three types of songs remain popular today, it may be helpful to describe each one in greater detail.

Psalm singing has a rich heritage in the Christian Church. The reading of the Psalms was a common practice in monasticism and was popular among the European Reformed Christians, some of whom still limit corporate song to the Psalms.[14] One reason for the popularity of the Psalms throughout the history of the Church is that they are the inspired words of God. As such, there is no better way to be assured that we are lovingly worshiping God in truth than by singing the Psalms.

The singing of Psalms seems to have diminished towards the end of the twentieth-century among mainline American Protestants but not among contemporary artists. Don Chaffer, for example, wrote a version of Psalm 125 called "Those Who Trust," a song recently recorded by *El Salvador*. The incomparable Richard Smallwood often draws from the deep well of the Psalms. Psalm 150 forms the foundation of his "Anthem of Praise," his "Great is the Lord" is subtitled Psalm 48, and his "I Love

---

12. Barth, *Church Dogmatics* IV.3.2, 866–67.
13. Bonhoeffer, *Life Together*, 58–61.
14. While biblical scholars have sound reason to refer to many passages in scripture as "psalms," there is also sound reason to use the word "Psalm" as a referent to the one hundred and fifty recorded in the Old Testament Psalter. For the sake of instructing the faithful, I have found it beneficial to apply the more narrow definition.

the Lord," recorded by the late Whitney Houston, echoes the cry of Psalm 116. Unlike the efforts of previous generations, contemporary Psalms repeat lyrics and usually don't include the entire Psalm in one song. The fruit of that approach, however, is that contemporary Psalms can be sung without notated music and easily learned by memory. The point, here, being that Psalm singing still characterizes the worship of God's people.

Hymn singing has been around since the first century. In fact, many Biblical scholars think the words of Philippians 2:5–11, which describe the humiliation of Christ, may be the lyric of a hymn sung by the early church. Hymn singing has been very popular among Protestants, especially since the days of Jonathan Edwards. Isaac Watts, a contemporary of Edwards, as well as a fellow Calvinist clergyman, paved the way for the popularity of hymns. He suggested that it was not necessary to limit congregational singing to exact biblical words, i.e., the Psalms. He offered as an alternative—the singing of song based on scriptural themes—by writing hymns for private devotional use and by publishing them as *Hymns and Spiritual Songs* in 1707.[15] Since Watts, countless hymns, like "Great Is Thy Faithfulness" and "How Great Thou Art," have been written and sung the world over by the Christian Church.

How shall we define a hymn? The Greek word *hymnos* refers to songs in praise of the gods or of a hero and, in that vein, Augustine defined a hymn as a song of praise to God. But a quick review of any hymn book demands a broader definition. Hughes Oliphant Olds and Stephen Marini help us here with descriptions that seem on target. Olds offers a content-driven definition of a hymn: "an elaboration, a sort of drawing out, a commentary, or perhaps a sort of meditation on the Lord and His Word."[16] Marini adds that a hymn must not only convey "belief content," but also be presented with "sacred intentionality;" it must serve a "ritual intention" or "defining purpose" in the liturgy.[17] In short, the lyrics of hymns commentate on biblical truth and when they elaborate on the greatness of our God, they provide a great vehicle by which to worship the Lord.

There is no consensus among students of Scripture and of the early church as to the exact nature of "Holy Spirit songs." Frank Senn suggests that they are "what people sing to one another for encouragement or to

---

15. See Marsden, *Jonathan Edwards*, 144.
16. Old, *Worship Reformed According to Scripture*, 39.
17. Marini, *Sacred Song in America*, 7.

express certain sentiments."[18] Gordon Fee suggests that they are songs inspired in the moment by the Holy Spirit. As noted earlier, his rational for this observation is that where the Spirit dwells, there is singing. Granted, some of the songs inspired in a moment do not have staying power, but some do. "These become the treasure-trove of our ongoing teaching and admonishing of one another, as well as of our constantly turning to God the Father and God the Son and offering praise by inspiration of the Holy Spirit."[19]

Closely related to the song inspired in the moment, is an improvisational form of song. Not long ago I had the privilege of sitting in a workshop led by Kevin Singleton, a gifted song writer and musician from New York. In this particular session, he taught worship leaders how to "go with the flow" by playing a three chord progression over and over. While playing the progression, he sang a new song, a short "diddy" (as some call it). I watched with amazement as, in the moment, he taught it to his choir (with harmonies), and then taught it to the congregation. What would you call that? How would you label that type of song? Seems like a Holy Spirit song to me—one that merges the musical gifts of the musician with a word from the Lord.

Others believe that spiritual songs may be understood as spontaneous singing which may or may not be prophetic or poetic. We find an example of the prophetic in the Old Testament. After Saul was chosen to be the first king, he received an order from Samuel to meet with "a company of prophets" and join them in their prophesying. When the people saw him sitting with the prophets and singing psalms in their midst, they asked with surprise: "Is Saul also among the Prophets?" (1 Kgs 10:11–2).

Personally, I wonder if Paul was referring to "scripture songs," those simple tunes we write to accompany the words of Scripture (other than the Psalms). Might "spiritual songs" be similar to the songs we create to teach children the stories of Scripture? Like the story of *Zaccheus* that "wee little man" who "climbed into a sycamore tree?" Could "spiritual songs" refer to those short choruses, like the *Kyrie eleison*, which teach, by repeated use, the word of the Lord? If these songs are not "spiritual songs," then they surely represent a fourth type of song common among Christians: the Scripture song.

---

18. Senn, *Introduction to Christian Liturgy*, 177.
19. Fee, *Paul, the Spirit, and the People of God*, 159.

In recent years, American Protestants, and perhaps others, have experienced a truly remarkable explosion of spiritual or scripture songs. American Evangelicals typically classify them as "praise and worship" songs. This type of song now dominates the worship of American Evangelicals, is making its way into the worship of African Americans, and has seeped into traditional forms of worship practiced by other Protestants. When compared to psalms and hymns, this type of sacred song is characterized by simplicity, redundancy, and a lower density of information. While many find those qualities reason enough to minimize their use in worship, Hughes Oliphant Olds offers this more balanced perspective:

> It is of the very nature of American Protestantism that the ministry of praise is so central to its worship and flows forth so abundantly and in such rich variety. This should not surprise us. We have often seen this happen before. The ministry of praise wells up from the grass roots of Christian faith. It is a folk art, inspired by the Holy Spirit, and comes naturally in its own time.[20]

The Styles of Music

Style differs from function and type. Style is a way of singing shaped by a particular person or group of people from a particular time and place. For that reason, music takes shape in countless styles. One day, years ago, I surfed an internet radio website that identified over 300 styles of music from which I could choose. That simple act of research pretty much shattered any hope I had up to that point in life for eclectic or "blended" corporate worship. Looking at that list, I realized that a congregation will never blend more than a few styles of music—nor will it want to. Instead, in the same manner a congregation selects a default language for worship, it will inevitably choose a default style by which it offers its praise in songs to the Beloved. The premise upon which I make that assertion is found in the growing field of ethnomusicology, a field wherein we find comparisons between language and music. Bruno Nettl writes, "Without pretending that language and music are of the same cloth, there are sufficient similarities to have permitted ethnomusicologists to take certain cues from the study of language."[21]

---

20. Old, *Worship Reformed According to Scripture*, 56–57.
21. Nettl, *Study of Ethnomusicology*, 56.

One of the similarities between language and music is that just as individuals have a heart language, they have a preferred style of music by which they share the matters of their hearts. For the sake of this conversation, let's refer to it as a "heart style." A person's heart language is the language he or she first learned. As noted in the previous chapter, it is the language one employs when praying about his or her deepest needs and concerns. A person's heart style is the type of music a person employs when praying through song about his or her deepest needs and concern. Like our heart language, our heart style is learned within a particular cultural context. Like our heart language, we draw upon our heart style to express love, joy, sorrow, and need. Like our heart language, we employ our heart style when loving our Beloved; it is the style by which we best worship the Lord in spirit and in truth. Surely we can worship the Lord with styles other than our heart style, but that worship falls short of our hopes and dreams. In order to love the Lord with heart, soul, mind, and strength—to worship authentically—when given a choice we will opt for our heart style of music. Then, and only then, do we feel like we have expressed our deepest longings and loves.[22]

If we accept the idea that a person has a heart style of music by which he or she worships the Lord with heart and soul, *then we may conclude that music style best not be viewed as a simply a preference*. It runs far deeper than personal preference. Along that same line of thinking, we may suggest that congregations typically select a particular style of music by which they express their love in song for their Beloved. Surely, those same congregations season their liturgies with other styles, but each congregation will default to a particular style. And we should expect as much.

By those assertions I do not negate the possibility of a Christ-follower or a congregation learning a new style—one that, over time, seeps into the very heart and soul of its congregants. Indeed, that happened to me. During the first thirty years of my life as a Christ-follower I loved to worship the Lord with traditional psalms and hymns, accompanied by organ. But half way through my journey, I was introduced to a new style—Black Gospel—and it has become my heart style. When expressing love for my Beloved, I borrow songs from the Cynthia Cymbala, Richard Smallwood, Donnie McClurkin, Clint Brown, and others like them. I suppose many

---

22. See, as an example, the role of "shout" in African American worship in Raboteau, *African-American Region*.

other Christ-followers have shared a similar experience, as have many congregations.

I also predict that there may come a time when I, like my father, will resist learning a new heart style of music. My dad was an organ-accompanied psalms and hymns kind of Christ-follower who gathered each week with a congregation of like-styled Christians. Throughout the latter years of his life he was encouraged by those in church leadership to abandon his heart style and learn another. Instead of baroque, organ–based music, he was to worship the Lord accompanied by a band of guitars and drums. The assumption behind the admonition he had received was that music style is merely a preference, a personal choice. The rationale for that same admonition was that the church needed to change its style of music for the sake of the extension of the Gospel to seekers. Now is not the time and place to discuss the process by which a congregation selects a style of music. Suffice it to note at this point that music style is more than a preference. Hence, when we change the style of music by which our congregants worship the Lord, we are asking them to learn another language. Hence, such decisions engender as much conflict as a proposal to change the language of the liturgy.

Another question, however, one that elicits the most passionate responses from my seminary students, is this: Are some styles of music more appropriate than others for worship? Based on the theory of heart style, some claim any style of music may accompany the praise and worship of people who, through song, worship their Beloved. Others, like Michael Horton, claim that "style is not neutral."[23] They believe that some styles of music are more appropriate than others for worship. By that assertion, they do not mean to suggest that some styles are morally suspect. In and of themselves, the styles are fine and good, just more appropriate for other venues, such as a concert, outdoor music festival, or an athletic contest. Those same styles, it is believed, fail to create adequate support for congregational song or fail to cultivate the kind of atmosphere that encourages worship of a loving and majestic God.

While I do not have enough expertise to appropriately articulate that reality, I know it to be true from personal experience. I have discovered that the music in an elevator differs from the music in a night club, the music in a restaurant differs from the music at a basketball game, the music of a sanctuary differs from that of a concert hall, and the music of

---

23. Horton, *A Better Way*, 163–87.

lovers differs from that of war. I am forced to conclude that the power of music discourages certain styles of music from finding their way into certain areas of life. Hence, I believe it safe to conclude that not all styles of music are appropriate for Christian worship. Yet I acknowledge the difficulty of quantifying that conviction. For good or ill, it seems we don't know until we try. In other words, we know what styles of music "work" from experience. I am not referring to the styles outside of the boundaries of the conversation, nor about the styles which form the center of the conversation. Those are obvious to all. I am referring to those styles that lie between the center and the boundaries: Jazz, Heavy Metal, Bluegrass, Hip-Hop, and others come to mind. The question raised by styles like these is, "Can they be used effectively and reverently in Christian worship?" It seems that when evaluating these styles and others, context will determine the appropriateness of a particular style: a unique context which lies between the style of song and the memory of the worshiper. A style of music, for example, may be so imbedded in the memory of the worshiper that it hinders, rather than promotes love for the Beloved. And the opposite may also be affirmed.

Making Music Work Today

During the past few decades, we have witnessed an explosion of sacred music, most of which is readily accessible to the people in the pews through radio and internet. At the same time, we have witnessed significant liturgical renewal throughout American Protestantism. Consequently, as we travel through the initial decades of a new century, countless sacred songs are available for use in worship. How do we navigate through all the options?

In the generations before us, denominations often provided this important service. They appointed task forces and committees to select songs and publish songbooks for use by their congregations. There was a time, in fact, when congregations limited their songs to those approved for such use by their denominations. While denominations continue to serve in that role, the denominational bureaucracy has not been able to keep up with the wave of new music published in the last four decades. Today, a hymn or song book is out of date the very date it is published.

Recognizing that new landscape, several scholars have come forward in recent years to provide helpful tools for those within local congregations who share the responsibility of selecting music for the weekly gatheringsGod's people. Thomas Long encourages congregations to emphasize "congregational music that is both excellent and eclectic in style and genre."[24] Marva Dawn suggests we ask the following questions before asking a congregation to sing a particular song:

1. Is the text of the song theologically sound?
2. Does the style of the song disrupt worship in any way?
3. How appropriate is the piece with respect to our goal to use music in support of the diversity of the congregation?
4. Is this piece of music characterized by excellence and greatness?[25]

Emily Brink and John Witvliet offer four guiding principles for the selection of liturgical music:

1. Music should serve to enact the relationship we have with God in Christ;
2. Music should be common to all the people;
3. Music should have theological integrity; and
4. Music should be in, but not of the culture of the people.[26]

Frank Burch Brown blends the aesthetic element with the selection of music for congregational singing. He offers a list of assumptions that could fruitfully guide a congregation's discussion about aesthetics and music. They could be enlarged, printed on a laminated poster board, and tacked to the wall of the appropriate church office.

1. There are many kinds of good religious art and music. In view of cultural diversity, it would be extremely odd if that were not true.
2. Not all kinds of good art and music are equally good for worship. It is not enough that a work or style of art be likeable; it must be appropriate.
3. There are various appropriately Christian modes of mediating religious experience artistically—from transcendent to immanent

---

24. Long, *Beyond the Worship Wars*, 60.
25. Dawn, *Reaching Out Without Dumbing Down*, 202.
26. Brink and Witvliet, "Music in Reformed Churches Worldwide," 339–47.

in a sense of the sacred, from abundant to minimal means, from prophetic to pastoral in tone; from instructive to meditative in aim.

4. Every era and cultural context develops new forms of sacred music and art, which to begin with often seem secular to many people.

5. No one person can make equally discerning judgments about every kind of music or art. Yet almost everyone is inclined to assume or act otherwise.

6. It is an act of Christian love to learn to appreciate or at least respect what others value in a particular style or work that they cherish in worship. That is different, however, from personally liking every form of commendable art, which is impossible and unnecessary.

7. Disagreements over taste in religious music or any other art can be healthy and productive; but they touch on sensitive matters and often reflect or embody religious differences as well as aesthetic and personal ones.

8. The reasons why an aesthetic work or style is good or bad, weak or strong, can never be expressed in words, yet they can often be pointed out through comparative—and repeated—looking and listening.

9. Aesthetic judgments begin with the community or tradition to which a given style or work is indigenous or most familiar. But they seldom end there; and they cannot, if the style or work is to invite the attention of a wide range of people over a period of time.

10. The overall evaluation of any art used in worship needs to be a joint effort between clergy, congregation, and trained artists and musicians, taking into account the aesthetic qualities of the art and the requirements of the liturgy.

11. The congregation benefits from "classic" art or music that challenges and solicits spiritual and theological growth in the aesthetic dimension.[27]

Finally, John Witvliet, building on the work of the legendary Robert Webber, proposes "categories for thinking about the valid and healthy use of music in the context of Christian worship."[28] He creatively introduces these categories through the use of questions:

---

27. Brown, *Good Taste, Bad Taste, and Christian Taste*, 250–51.
28. Witvliet, "Beyond Style," 71.

1. A Theological Question: Do we have the imagination and resolve to speak and make music in a way that both celebrates and limits the role of music as a conduit for experiencing God?[29]

2. A Liturgical Question: Do we have the imagination and persistence to develop and play music that enables and enacts the primary actions of Christian worship?

3. An Ecclesial Question: Do we have the imagination and persistence to make music that truly serves the gathered congregation, rather than the musicians, composer, or marketing company that promotes it?

4. An Aesthetic Question: Do we have the persistence and imagination to develop and then practice a rich understanding of "aesthetic virtue"?

5. A Cultural Question: Do we have a sufficiently complex understanding of the relationship between worship, music, and culture to account for how worship is at once trans-cultural, contextual, countercultural, and cross-cultural?

6. An Economic Question: Do we have the imagination and persistence to overcome deep divisions in the Christian church along the lines of socioeconomic class?[30]

In the end, it seems that we must lean on the Holy Spirit to grant us the gift of discernment in order that as a congregation, we may wisely employ those forms of music and song which both glorify our Triune God and remain consonant with our heart style and indigenous culture. Where aesthetic differences arise out of the generational or ethnic barriers, we must seek the grace to be sensitive to our brothers and sisters in Christ, knowing that such divisions are not the result of superficial preference, but instead are as fundamental as the question of whether we

---

29. Here John Witvliet explores a common misconception that music ushers a person in to the presence of God. He writes, "There is no doubt that music has great significance in the divine-human encounter of worship . . . But can we safely take the next step and believe that music generates an experience of God? By no means. That places far too much power in music itself. Music is not God, nor is music an automatic tool for generating God's presence . . . Music is an instrument by which the Holy Spirit draws us to God, a tool by which we enact our relationship with God. It is not a magical medium for conjuring up God's presence." See Witvliet, "Beyond Style," 71–72.

30. Ibid., 67–81.

conduct our service in English or French, Romanian or Dutch, Spanish or Swahili.

chapter 8

CONCLUSION

THE APOCALYPSE OF JOHN was not written for Christians enjoying a vacation aboard a luxurious cruise ship; it was written for believers experiencing suffering and tribulation. It was written for Christians unsure that God reigned supreme over the world. Its visions were meant to strengthen those believers while they suffered persecution from the hands of Rome. The fourth and fifth chapters, in particular, encouraged perplexed believers with a beautiful vision of the sovereignty of God. The vision conveyed in those chapters taught the infant Church that, no matter what she endured on the earth, she should never forget that God reigns in majesty. In the midst of tribulation, she should gaze upon the One who is King of Kings and Lord of Lords. That beautiful vision includes a picture of worship by the church triumphant. The setting for that ecclesiastical service is heaven, where we find God the Father sitting on a throne. John compares his appearance to two precious and radiant jewels: jasper and carnelian (4:3). A large and diverse congregation worships God the Father, a group that includes four striking creatures who may represent all living creatures. It also includes the community of the redeemed, represented by twenty-four elders wearing garments of holiness and crowns of victory. The Elders may also represent the twelve patriarchs of the Old Testament era and the twelve apostles of the New Testament period (Rev 21:12,14).

But there is more. Without explanation, both God the Father and the Lamb of God inhabit the heavenly throne. The Lamb represents none other than Jesus Christ, the triumphant Redeemer who, with the Father, governs the entire universe (Eph 1:22–23). His seven horns and seven eyes symbolize his complete authority, omnipotence, and omnipresence. The congregation, including countless angels, worships the Lamb, singing, "Worthy is the Lamb, who was slain, to receive power and wealth and wisdom and strength and honor and glory and praise" (Revelation 5:12). That worship serves as but a prelude to the "praise and honor and glory and power" rendered by every creature in heaven and on earth and under the earth and on the sea.

Such is the future of the redeemed. One day we will join the heavenly hosts in perpetual worship of our God. Until that time, we, the militant church, the imperfect church, the adulterous bride of Christ, worship the Lord with our frail voices, divided attentions, limited understandings, and nagging sins. We do so trusting that God the Holy Spirit will compensate for our weaknesses and, thereby, enable us to worship in spirit and in truth. We also do so trusting that, while worship is first and foremost about the Lord, during our hour or so with God's people, the Holy Spirit will shape us, improve us, motivate us, do something in, for, and through us.

We hold firm to such faith, longing to leave God's gathered community different than we arrived, though we seldom have objective proof to confirm such an experience. Occasionally, for sure, our worship seems heavenly and we leave the gathered community saying, "It's been good to be in the house of the Lord." Like Jacob who wrestled with God, we come away from "church" convinced that we experienced a genuine encounter with the Lord. Frustrated by the infrequencies of such experiences we may question the authenticity of our worship. Such inquiries, however, flow from our fleeting feelings and seldom represent reality. God works mysteriously and, sometimes, imperceptibly. Whether we feel it or not, we believe (O God, help our unbelief!) that the proclaimed Word impacts us. As Isaiah recorded, "As the rain and the snow come down from heaven, and do not return to it without watering the earth and making it bud and flourish, so that it yields seed for the sower and bread for the eater, so is my word that goes out from my mouth: It will not return to me empty, but will accomplish what I desire and achieve the purpose for which I sent it" (55:10–11). Hence, while our feelings may lead us to conclude that "we got nothing out of a service," God's Word leads us to conclude otherwise.

While affirming that God's grace is sufficient to compensate for our limitations and sins regarding worship, we also cooperate with the Holy Spirit and work at our worship. We circumspectly review our services to determine when and where we, like the Ephesians, have left our first love (Rev 2:4). We periodically review our liturgical practices and discover, as should be expected, that our liturgies have been shaped, to one degree or another, by preferences and prejudices, rather than by biblical or theological principles. These deficiencies don't alarm us, for we know we are sinners prone to idolatry, but they disappoint us. We hope for better out of ourselves. We truly desire to love the Lord with our worship. So, after confessing our waywardness, we work at our worship, seeking to minimize the liturgical influence of our weaknesses, while at the same time maximizing the grace and grandeur of the one we worship.

That work will be built on the indisputable convictions that the shape of a lover's love shall be determined by the beloved, not by the lover, and that worship is the loving response of individuals and congregations to the love of the Triune God, our Beloved. In other words, our worship shall be regulated by our Beloved. In a manner of speaking, it shall be shaped by the heart of our Triune God. Upon the foundation of those statements, in this volume I have attempted to assist those responsible for planning the weekly gatherings of God's people. In the process, I have not provided a check list of dos and don'ts. Instead, I have sought to identify biblical principles that reflect the heart of God and influence how we love the Lord in worship. In short, I have offered a biblical theology for worship. As such, it invites readers to not only affirm biblical principles, but engage in the difficult task of contextualizing each one.

Thankfully, one day we will not have to work at our worship. As foretold in Revelation 21, we will dwell in the new heaven and the new earth. We will worship in the New Jerusalem. John's beautiful, vivid, and detailed description of that Holy City, however, has led some to miss a very important truth. The New Jerusalem is not a place, but a people. It is not the final home of the redeemed; it is the redeemed. The New Jerusalem is a symbol of the bride, the church. It is a real and precious community of individuals who have direct and immediate fellowship with God. In heaven, we will be his people; God himself will be with us and be our God (21:3). Until then, we will continue reflecting on how best to love our Beloved through worship. We will study and evaluate, pray and plan, confess and praise. We will, as someone once said, "do our best and let God do the rest."

In the time between now and our eternal worship of our Beloved, let us grant to others the grace our Triune God grants to us. May we be patient with the perceived shortcomings of fellow Christians who don't love as we think they should love and, thereby, don't worship the way we think they should worship. (After all, who among us wants to be the one who criticizes the amount of oil or price of perfume poured out in worship?) May the Lord also grant us humility to recognize that, even following our best efforts, our liturgical practices will always reflect our shortcomings and sins. There will always be something about our convictions today that embarrass us tomorrow. There will always be times when we look back at our lives and wonder "What was I thinking?" So at this time in our pilgrimage, let us ask the Lord to grant us courage to identify and forsake our idols, as well as wisdom to discern his good and perfect will. May he so do until that day we won't have to work at worship, until that day we join the redeemed, as well as all living creatures, in perpetual praise to our Beloved.

BIBLIOGRAPHY

Allen, Horace T. Jr. "Calendar and Lectionary in Reformed Perspective and History." In *Christian Worship in Reformed Churches Past and Present*, edited by Lukas Vischer. Sun, et al., 390–414. Grand Rapids, MI: Eerdmans, 2003.
Anderson, E. Byron. "'O for a heart to praise my God': Hymning the Self Before God." In *Liturgy and the Moral Self*, edited by E Byron Anderson and Bruce T. Morrill. Sun, et al., 111–26. Collegeville, MN: The Liturgical, 1998.
Appleton, George, ed. *The Oxford Book of Prayer*. Oxford University Press, 1985.
Aumann, Jordon. *Christian Spirituality in the Catholic Tradition*. San Francisco, CA: Ignatius, 1985.
Authentic Worship in a Changing Culture. Grand Rapids, MI: CRC, 1997.
Balswick, Jack O. and Judy K. Balswick. *The Family: A Christian Perspective on the Contemporary Home*. Grand Rapids, MI: Baker, 1999.
Barth, Karl. *Church Dogmatics*. London: T&T Clark, 1961.
Bass, Dorothy, ed. *Practicing Our Faith: A Way of Life for a Searching People*. San Francisco: Jossey-Bass, 2010.
Bass, Dorothy and Susan Briehl, eds. *On Our Way: Practices for Living a Whole Life*. Nashville, TN: Upper Room, 2010.
Bebbington, David. *Evangelicalism in Modern Britain*. Routledge, 1989.
Bierma, Nathan. "Keeping Holy Ground Holy." *Christianity Today* 53:5 (2009) 36.
Bloesch, Donald. *Church: Sacraments, Worship, Ministry, Mission*. Downers Grove, IL: InterVarsity, 2002.
———. *The Holy Spirit: Works and Gifts*. Downers Grove, IL: InterVarsity, 2005.
Bonhoeffer, Dietrich. *Life Together*. New York: Harper & Row, 1954.
Borgmann, Albert. *Power Failure: Christianity in the Culture of Technology*. Grand Rapids, MI: Brazos, 2003.
Breen, Mike and Steve Cochran. *Developing a Discipleship Culture*. Grand Rapids, MI: Zondervan, 2011.
Brimlow, Robert W. "Solomon's Porch: The Church as Sectarian Ghetto." In *The Church as Counterculture*, edited by Michael L. Budde and Robert W. Brimlow. Sun, et al., 105–26. Albany, NY: State University of New York Press, 2000.
Brink, Emily R. and John D. Witvliet. "Music in Reformed Churches Worldwide." In *Christian Worship in Reformed Churches Past and Present*, edited by Lukas Vischer. Sun, et al., 324–57. Grand Rapids, MI: Eerdmans, 2003.

BIBLIOGRAPHY

Brown, Frank Burch. *Good Taste, Bad Taste, and Christian Taste: Aesthetics in the Religious Life*. New York: Oxford University Press, 2000.
Bruggink, Donald J. and Carl H. Droppers. *Christ and Architecture: Building Presbyterian/Reformed Churches*. Grand Rapids, MI: William B. Eerdmans, 1965.
Budde, Michael L. and Robert W. Brimlow, eds. *The Church as Counterculture*. Albany, NY: State University of New York Press, 2000.
Burghardt, Walter J. *Christ in Ten Thousand Places*. Mahwah, NJ: Paulist, 1999.
Burkhart, John. *Worship: A Searching Examination of the Liturgical Experience*. Louisville, KY: Westminster John Knox, 1982.
Calvin, John. *Institutes of the Christian Religion*, 2 vols. Translated by Ford Lewis Battles, edited by John T. McNeill. Philadelphia: Westminster, 1960.
———. *The Necessity of Reforming the Church*. Protestant Heritage, 1995.
Carey, Philip. *Good News for Anxious Christians: 10 Practical Things You Don't Have to Do*. Grand Rapids, MI: Brazos, 2010.
Carothers, Merlin R. *Power in Praise*. Escondido, CA, 1972.
Carson, D.A., ed. *Worship by the Book*. Grand Rapids, MI: Zondervan, 2002.
Cavanaugh, William T. *Theological Imagination: Christian Practices in Space and Time*. New York: Bloomsbury, 2003.
Chan, Simon. *Liturgical Theology: The Church as a Worshiping Community*. Downers Grove, IL: InterVarsity, 2006.
Chapman, Gary. *The 5 Love Languages: The Secret to Love That Lasts*. Grand Rapids, MI: Zondervan, 1992.
Chapell, Bryan. *Christ-Centered Worship: Letting the Gospel Shape Our Practice*. Grand Rapids, MI: Baker Academic, 2009.
Cherry, Constance. *The Worship Architect: A Blueprint for Designing Culturally Relevant and Biblically Faithful Services*. Grand Rapids, MI: Baker, 2010.
Clapp, Rodney. *A Peculiar People: The Church as Culture in a Post-Christian Society*. Downers Grove, IL: InterVarsity, 1996.
Clowney, Edmund P. *The Church*. Downers Grove, IL: InterVarsity, 1995.
Dawn, Marva. *A Royal "Waste" of Time: The Splendor of Worshiping God and Being Church for the World*. Grand Rapids, MI: Eerdmans, 1999.
———. *Reaching Out Without Dumbing Down: A Theology of Worship for the Turn-Of-The-Century Culture*. Grand Rapids, MI: Eerdmans, 1995.
de Gruchy, John W. "Holy Beauty: A Reformed Perspective on Aesthetics within a World of Ugly Injustice." In *Reformed Theology for the Third Christian Millennium: The 2001 Sprunt Lectures.*, edited by B.A. Gerrish. Sun, et al., 13–26. Westminster John Knox, 2003.
Dobson, Edward G. *Starting a Seeker-Sensitive Service*. Grand Rapids, MI: Zondervan, 1993.
Dominy, Bert. "Spirit, Church, and Mission: Theological Implication of Pentecost." *Southwestern Journal of Theology* 35:2 (1993) 34–39.
Dyrness, William A. *A Primer on Christian Worship*. Grand Rapids, MI: Eerdmans, 2009.
———. *Visual Faith: Art, Theology, and Worship in Dialogue*. Grand Rapids, MI: Baker, 2001.
Edwards, Jonathan. *Charity and its Fruits: Christian Love as Manifested in the Heart and Life*. 1605. Reprint, Carlisle, PA: Banner of Truth Trust, 1969.
———. *A Treatise Concerning Religious Affections in Three Parts*. 1746.

Farley, Michael A. "What is 'Biblical Worship'? Biblical Hermeneutics and Evangelical Theologies of Worship." *Journal of the Evangelical Theological Society* (September 2008) 592–601.

Fee, Gordon D. *Paul, the Spirit, and the People of God.* Peabody, MA: Hendrickson, 1996.

Fernandez, Eleazar S. "From Babel to Pentecost: Finding a Home in the Belly of the Empire." *Semeia* 90–91 (2002) 29–50.

Fitch, David. *The Great Giveaway: Reclaiming the Mission of the Church from Big Business, Parachurch Organizations, Psychotherapy, Consumer Capitalism, and Other Modern Maladies.* Grand Rapids, MI: Baker, 2005.

Foster, Richard. *Prayer: Finding the Heart's True Home.* New York: HarperCollins, 1992.

Fromont, Paul. *Belonging and Not Belonging: The Creative Margins.* http://theminorkeys.blogspot.com/2013/08/belonging-and-not-belonging-creative.html.

Geddy, Welton. *The Gift of Worship.* Nashville, TN: Broadman, 1992.

Gonzalez, Justo L. *The Healing of the Nations: The Book of Revelation in an Age of Cultural Conflict.* Maryknoll, New York: Orbis, 1999.

Haidt, Jonathan. *The Righteous Mind: Why Good People are Divided by Politics and Religion.* New York, NY: Pantheon, 2012.

Hageman, Howard. *Pulpit and Table.* Richmond, Virginia: John Knox, 1962.

Hamstra, Sam, Jr. "The Americanization of the Church and Its Pastoral Ministry." *The New Mercersburg Review* (Spring 1992) 3–19.

———. "An Idealist View of Revelation." In *Four Views of Revelation*, edited by Marvin C. Pate. Sun, et al., 93–132. Grand Rapids, MI: Zondervan, 1997.

———. *Principled Worship: Biblical Roots for Emerging Liturgies.* Eugene, OR: Wipf & Stock, 2006.

———, ed. *The Reformed Pastor: Lectures on Pastoral Theology by John Nevin.* Eugene, OR: Pickwick, 2006.

Hart, D.G., and John R. Muether. *With Reverence and Awe: Returning to the Basics of Reformed Worship.* Phillipsburg, New Jersey: P&R, 2002.

Hauerwas, Stanley. *Community of Character: Toward a Constructive Christian Social Ethic.* University of Notre Dame Press, 1981.

Henry, Carl H. *Twilight of a Great Civilization: The Drift Toward Neo-Paganism.* Westchester, IL: Crossway, 1988.

Horton, Michael. *A Better Way: Rediscovering the Drama of Christ-Centered Worship.* Grand Rapids, MI: Baker, 2002.

Hovda, Robert. "Pentecost: Distinctive Cultures and Common Prayer." *Worship* 62 (1988) 260–65.

Howard, Evan B. *The Brazos Introduction to Christian Spirituality.* Grand Rapids, MI: Brazos, 2008.

Huyser-Honig, Joan. "Ethnodoxology: Calling all peoples to worship in their heart language." www.worship.calvin.edu/resources/resource-library.

Hybels, Bill. *Courageous Leadership.* Grand Rapids, MI: Zondervan, 2002.

Job, Rueben P. *Three Simple Rules: A Wesleyan Way of Living.* Nashville, TN: Abingdon, 2007.

Johnson, Todd, ed. *The Conviction of Things Not Seen: Worship and Ministry in the 21st Century.* Grand Rapids, MI: Brazos, 2002.

Jüngel, Eberhard. "Trinitarian Prayers for Christian Worship." Translated by Frederick J. Gaise. *Word & World.* XVIII:3 (1998) 244–53.

Kittel, Gerhard, and Gerhard Friedrich. *Theological Dictionary of the New Testament.* Grand Rapids, MI: Eerdmans, 1976.

Kreeft, Peter. *Back to Virtue: Traditional Moral Wisdom for Modern Moral Confusion.* San Francisco, CA: Ignatius, 1992.

Küng, Hans. *The Church.* Garden City, NY: Image, 1976.

Kuyper, Abraham. *The Work of the Holy Spirit.* Grand Rapids, MI: Eerdmans, 1979.

Lee, Jung Young. *Marginality: The Key to Multi-Cultural Theology.* Minneapolis, MN: Fortress, 1995.

Leonard, Richard C. "Music and Worship in the Bible," http://www.laudemont.org/a-mawitb.htm.

"Liturgical Committee Report." *Acts of Synod of the Christian Reformed Church.* Grand Rapids, MI: Christian Reformed Church, 1968.

Long, Thomas G. *Beyond the Worship Wars: Building Vital and Faithful Worship.* The Alban Institute, 2001.

Marini, Stephen A. *Sacred Song in America: Religion, Music, and Public Culture.* Chicago, IL: University of Illinois Press, 2003.

Marsden, George. *Jonathan Edwards A Life.* New Haven: Yale University Press, 2003.

Marshall, Paul, with Lela Gilbert. *Their Blood Cries Out: The Worldwide Tragedy of Modern Christians Who Are Dying for Their Faith.* Dallas, TX: Word, 1997.

Martin, Ralph. *The Worship of God: Some Theological Pastoral, and Practical Reflections.* Grand Rapids, MI: Eerdmans, 1982.

McKee, Elsie Anne, ed. *John Calvin: Writings on Pastoral Piety (Classics of Western Spirituality).* New York: Paulist, 2001.

———. "Reformed Worship in the Sixteenth Century." *Christian Worship in Reformed Churches Past and Present,* edited by Lukas Vischer. Sun, et al., 3–31. Grand Rapids, MI: Eerdmans, 2003.

McKnight, John. *The Careless Society.* New York: Basic, 1995.

Meeks, Wayne A. *The First Urban Christians: The Social World of the Apostle Paul.* New Haven: Yale University Press, 1983.

Merriam, Alan P. *The Anthropology of Music.* Evanston, IL: Northwestern University Press, 1964.

Morgenthaler, Sally. *Worship Evangelism.* Grand Rapids, MI: Zondervan, 1999.

Mouw, Richard. *He Shines in All That's Fair.* Grand Rapids, MI: Eerdmans, 2001.

Nettl, Bruno. *Study of Ethnomusicology.* Chicago: University of Illinois Press, 2005.

Nevin, John Williamson. *The Mystical Presence and the Doctrine of the Reformed Church on the Lord's Supper.* 1846. Reprint edited by Linden J. DeBie. Eugene, OR: Wipf & Stock, 2012.

Newbegin, Lesslie. *The Household of God.* New York: Friendship, 1953.

Niebuhr, H. Reinhold. *Christ and Culture.* New York: Harper and Row, 1951.

Noll, Mark A. *Old Religion in a New World: The History of North American Christianity.* Grand Rapids, MI: Eerdmans, 2001.

Old, Hughes Oliphant. *Worship Reformed According to Scripture.* Louisville, KY: Westminster John Knox, 2002.

Patzschke, Theresa. "Empathy Towards the Performer Intensifies Music-Induced Emotion." http://www.united-academics.org/magazine/sex-society/empathy-towards-the-performer-intensifies-music-induced-emotion/.

Peterson, David. *Engaging with God: A Biblical Theology of Worship.* Downers Grove, IL: InterVarsity, 1992.

Piper, John. *Desiring God: Meditations of a Christian Hedonist*. Sisters, Oregon: Multnomah, 1986.
Postman, Neil. *Technopoly: The Surrender of Culture to Technology*. New York, NY: Vantage, 1992.
Psalter Hymnal. Grand Rapids,. MI: CRC, 1987.
Quicke, Michael. *Preaching as Worship: An Integrative Approach to Formation in Your Church*. Baker: Grand Rapids, MI, 2011.
Raboteau, Albert J. *African-American Religion*. New York: Oxford University Press, 1999.
Rice, Howard L. and James C. Huffstutler. *Reformed Worship*. Louisville, KY: Geneva, 2001.
Ross, Allen. *Recalling the Hope of Glory*. Grand Rapids, MI: Kregel, 2006.
Roszak, Theodor. *The Making of a Counter Culture: Reflections on the Technocratic Society and its Youthful Opposition*. New York: Doubleday and Company, 1969.
Schmemann, Alexander. *For the Life of the World*: Sacraments and Orthodoxy. Crestwood, NY: St. Vladimir's Seminary, 2002.
Schultze, Quentin J. *High-Tech Worship: Using Presentational Technologies Wisely*. Grand Rapids, MI: Baker, 2004.
Segler, Frankin. *Understanding, Preparing for, and Practicing Christian Worship*. 2nd Edition, revised by C. Randall Bradley. Nashville, TN: Broadman and Holman, 1996.
Senn, Frank. *Introduction to Christian Liturgy*. Minneapolis, MN: Fortress, 2012.
Smith, James K.A. *Desiring the Kingdom: Worship, Worldview, and Cultural Formation*. Grand Rapids, MI: Baker, 2009.
Stackhouse, John, ed. *What Does It Mean To be Saved?*. Grand Rapids, MI: Baker Academic, 2002.
Stanton, Gerald B. "Praise." In *Evangelical Dictionary of Theology*, edited by Walter A. Elwell. Sun, et al., 865–66. Grand Rapids, MI: Baker, 2001.
Strobel, Lee and Bill Hybels. *Inside the Mind of Unchurched Harry and Mary*. Grand Rapids, MI: Zondervan, 1993.
Suurmond, Jean-Jaques. *Word and Spirit at Play: Towards a Charismatic Theology*. Grand Rapids, MI: Eerdmans, 1995.
Temple, D. William. *The Hope of a New World*. 1942. Reprint, Kessinger, 2010.
The Liturgy of the Reformed Church in America. New York: Board of Education, 1968.
Thomas, Gary. *Sacred Pathways: Discover Your Soul's Path to God*. Grand Rapids, MI: Zondervan, 2000.
Torrance, James Torrance. *Worship, Community and the Triune God of Grace*. Downers Grove, IL: InterVarsity, 1996.
Tozer, A. W. *The Best of A.W. Tozer*. Grand Rapids, MI: Baker, 1978.
———. *The Knowledge of the Holy*. New York: Harper & Row, 1961.
Vann, Jane Rogers. *Gathered Before God: Worship-Centered Church Renewal*. Louisville, KY: John Knox, 2004.
Vischer, Lukas, ed. *Christian Worship in Reformed Churches Past and Present*. Grand Rapids, MI: Eerdmans, 2003.
Wainwright, Geoffrey and Karen B. Westerfield, eds. *The Oxford History of Christian Worship*. New York: Oxford University Press, 2006.
Wangerin, Walter Jr. *Preparing for Jesus*. Grand Rapids, MI: Zondervan, 1999.

Watts, Rick E. "The New Exodus/New Creational Restoration of the Image of God." In *What Does It Mean to be Saved?*, edited by John G. Stackhouse Jr. Grand Rapids, MI: Baker Academic, 2002.

Webber, Robert. *Ancient-Future Faith: Rethinking Evangelicalism for a Postmodern World.* Grand Rapids, MI: Baker, 1999.

———. *Divine Embrace: Recovering the Passionate Spiritual Life.* Grand Rapids, MI: Baker, 2006.

———. *Worship Old and New.* Revised ed. Grand Rapids, MI: Zondervan, 1994.

Wegner, Paul D. *The Journey from Texts to Translations: The Origin and Development of the Bible.* Grand Rapids, MI: Baker, 2004.

Wesley, John. "Thoughts on the Power of Music." In *John Wesley's Teachings Volume Three: Pastoral Theology*, edited by Thomas C. Oden. Grand Rapids, MI: Zondervan, 2013.

White, James. *Introduction to Christian Worship.* Nashville, TN: Abingdon, 1980.

White, Susan. *Foundations of Christian Worship.* Louisville, KY: Westminster John Knox, 2006.

Wilken, Robert. *The Spirit of Early Christian Thought.* New Haven, CT: Yale University Press, 2003.

Willard, Dallas. *Divine Conspiracy.* San Francisco, CA: HarperCollins, 1966.

———. *The Great Omission: Reclaiming Jesus' Essential Teachings on Discipleship.* San Francisco, CA: HarperCollins, 2006.

———. "The Human Body and Spiritual Growth." In *Christian Educator's Handbook on Spiritual Formation*, eds. Kenneth O. Gangel and James C. Wilhoit. Sun, et al., 225–33. Grand Rapids, MI: Baker, 1994.

———. *Renovation of the Heart: Putting on the Character of Christ.* Colorado Springs, CO: NavPress, 2002.

———. *The Spirit of the Disciplines: Understanding How God Changes Lives.* New York: HarperCollins, 1998.

Witvliet, John D. "Beyond Style." In *The Conviction of Things Not Seen: Worship and Ministry in the 21st Century*, edited by Todd Johnson. Sun, et al., 67–81. Grand Rapids, MI: Brazos, 2002.

———. *Worship Seeking Understanding: Windows into Christian Practice.* Grand Rapids, MI: Baker, 2003.

Wolters, Albert M. *Creation Regained: Biblical Basics for a Reformational Worldview.* Grand Rapids, MI: Eerdmans, 1985.

Wood, David. "Prime Time: Albert Borgmann on Taming Technology." *Christian Century* 120:17 (2003) 22–25.

The Worship Sourcebook. Grand Rapids, MI: Baker, 2004.

Wright, Christopher J. H. *The Mission of God: Unlocking the Bible's Grand Narrative.* Downers Grove, IL: InterVarsity, 2006.

Wright, N.T. Wright. *For All God's Worth: True Worship and the Calling of the Church.* Grand Rapids, MI: Eerdmans, 1997.

Author Index

Anderson, E. Byron, 80
Appleton, George, *Oxford Book of Prayer*, 83
Augustine, 50, 58, 128
Aumann, Jordon, 11, 59

Barth, Karl, 127
Beane, Marian, American values list, 97
Bierma, Nathan, 108
Bilizekian, Gilbert, 60
Bloesch, Donald, 13, 30–31, 84
Bonhoeffer, Dietrich, 57, 127
Borgmann, Albert, *Power Failure: Christianity in the Culture of Technology*, 117–118
Brimlow, Robert, 104
Brink, Emily, 134
Britten, Terry, 1
Brown, Frank Burch, 134–135
Bruggink, Donald, *Christ and Architecture*, 108
Brunner, Peter, 14
Burghardt, Walter, 53
Burkhart, John, 14

Calvin, John, 7, 29, 84, 92, 124
Campbell, Thomas, 126
Chaffer, Don, 127
Chan, Simon, 9, 13, 14, 27
Clapp, Rodney, 60, 105
Clowney, Edmund, 8

Dawn, Marva, 117, 134
De Gruchy, John, 114
Droppers, Carl, *Christ and Architecture*, 108
Dyrness, William, 30, 110

Edwards, Jonathan, 36, 43, 46, 84, 128

Farley, Michael, 7
Fee, Gordon, 124, 129
Foster, Richard, 44
Fosters, Richard, 44
Fromont, Paul, 15–16

Geddy, Welton, 14
Gonzalez, Justo, 75

Haidt, Jonathan, 38
Hauerwas, Stanley, 99
Henry, Carl F.H., 96
Hine, Stuart Keene, "How Great Thou Art," 48
Horton, Michael, 132
Hybels, Bill, xii

Job, Rueben, 59
Jüngel, Eberhard, 33

Kreeft, Peter, 46
Küng, Hans, 66, 73
Kuyper, Abraham, 30

Lehman, Frederick M., 49

Long, Thomas, 21, 134
Worship Wars, 109
Lyle, Graham Hamilton, 1

Marini, Stephen, 128
Marshall, Paul, *Their Blood Cries Out*, 106–107
Martin, Ralph, 14
McKee, Elsie, 7
Merriam, Alan P., 125–126
Mouw, Rich, 74

Nettl, Bruno, 121, 130
Nevin, John, 69, 71, 92
Newbigin, Lesslie, 27, 68
Niebuhr, H. Richard, 97

Old, Hughes Oliphant, 20, 128, 130

Paul, 2, 6, 27–28, 28, 45–46, 63, 99
on absence of love, 5
on love, 59
on response to God's love, 61
Peter, 53, 55, 73
Peterson, David, 9
Piper, John, 14, 47–48, 49
Pliny, 25
Post, Andrew, 90–91

Quicke, Michael, 48

Ross, Allen, 9
Roszak, Theodore, 119

Saletan, William, 38
Schmemann, Alexander, 9
Schultze, Quentin, *High Tech Worship*, 116–119
Segler, Franklin, 14
Senn, Frank, 11, 12, 13, 128
Singleton, Kevin, 129
Smallwood, Richard, 127
Smith, James K.A., 38, 78
Suurmond, Jean-Jacques, 28, 30

Temple, D. William, 14
Thomas, Gary, *Sacred Pathways*, 35–36
Torrance, James, 14, 24–25
Tozer, A.W., 21–22, 24
The Knowledge of the Holy, 79

Updike, John, "Seven Stanzas at Easter," 40–41

Vann, Jane, 36
Vischer, Lukas, 8, 100

Wainwright, Geoffrey, 9, 21
Wangerin, Walt, 22
Watts, Isaac, 128
Webber, Robert, xii, 9, 13, 14, 108, 135
Wegner, Paul, 101
Wesley, Charles, 126
White, James, 12, 14
Willard, Dallas, 29, 41–42, 49, 82, 88
Witvliet, John, 122, 134, 135, 136n29
Wolters, Al, 115
Wright, N.T., 36, 71–72

Scripture Index

Genesis
1:26	19, 21, 115
2:9	110
2:15	115
3:6	110
4:21	121
12:1	53
12:1-3	73, 95
14	86
28:22	86

Exodus
3:12	15
15:1-2	79
15:20-21	123
20:1-11	6
Leviticus	6, 23–24
10	6
19	59
Numbers 16	6

Deuteronomy
6	59
6:4	18
32	18
	Joshua
24:14-15	42
	Judges
5	123

1 Samuel
2	6, 80
10:5	123
25:31	43

2 Samuel
6	3–4
24:24	117
68	47

1 Kings
10:11-12	129

1 Chronicles
34	18
34:3	18
	Job
9:33, 35	24
27:6	43

Psalms
	6
4:7	126
8:3-4, 9	20
27:4	23
30:11-12	47
32-11	47
34:3	79
37:4	47

Psalms (cont.)

47:1	126
48	127
50:9-12	87
50:10	107
63	82
63:4	126
68	47
84:10	80
95:1-3	123
95:6	109
100	80
113	23
116	128
116:1-2	49
116:12-14	50
125	127
145	80
149:3	126
150	127

Isaiah

6:5	24, 83
6:5,6-7	84
19	73–74
26:1-6	123
29:13	3
38:20	124
53:5	91
54:1-6	49
55:10-11	139
58	6

Jeremiah

31:33	54n5
33:10-11	6

Lamentations

5:14	124

Ezekiel

26:13	124
33:32	123–124

Daniel

3:1-11	123

Zephaniah

3:17	124

Matthew

2:11	22
5:23-24	64
6:1-4	6, 88
7:21-23	68, 69
14:23	55
22:37-39	2, 59
23	82
26:6-12	117
28:19	73
28:19-20	74, 95

Mark

12:30	57
12:41	86
12:41-43	88
14:3-9	86
16:9-20	75

Luke

1:46-47	22
2:9-12	22
7:36-50	85
7:37-39	18
12:1	80
19:8	86
19:10	74, 95
24:48-53	75

John

3:16	19, 74, 91
4:10	94
4:23,24	54n5
7:38	59
10:17-18	19
13:34-35	59
15:9-12	59
16:5-15	28

17:14	99
17:14-16	99
17:20-21	63
17:21	61
20:19-26	89

Acts

2	60
2:32	19
8:38	73
10:4	81
13:2	11
20:7	89

Romans

1:4	19
1:18-23	20
3:10-18	70
8:6	19
8:11	41
8:15	29
8:26-27	29
9:4	13
12:1	13, 34, 42, 87
12:1-2	41
12:10	61
12:15	62
12:16	61
14:5	90
14:6	90
14:12	61
15:7	61
15:14	61
16:16	61

1 Corinthians

	58
1:10	61
1:26-31	54
3:16	28, 68
6:19	27
10:17	92
11:27-28	93
11:29	93
12:7	27
12:7-11	30
12:13	27, 29, 72
13:1	45, 61
13:13	45
14	30
16:2	87

2 Corinthians

4:6	28
8:5	86
9:5-6	88
9:6-7	87
12:9	45
13:14	19

Galatians

5:13	61
6:10	58

Ephesians

1:6	22
1:22-23	139
2:19	99
3:19	31
4:2	61
4:3	63
4:4-6	63, 88
4:4-7	59
4:12	27
4:30	28
4:32	61
5:17	123
5:19	61
5:21	61
6:10-20	99
6:17	29

Philippians

2:5-8	86
2:5-11	128
2:7	19
3:10	41
4:13	45

Colossians

3:16	61, 127

1 Thessalonians
5:11	61

1 Timothy
2:8	126

Hebrews
	24
4:14-16	25, 45
4:16	27
8:6	11
8:8	54n5
9:1, 6	13
10:19	25
10:25	66
12:11	47
14	25

James
1:17	82, 124
3:9-12	57–58

1 Peter
2:9	22, 55, 67, 79, 95
2:9-10	53–54, 96, 120
3:18	73
5:5-6	47

1 John
2:15-18	99
3:24	27
4:4	45
4:7-12	58

2 John
5-6	58

Revelation
	138–140
2:4	140
4:3	138
5:9-10	74
5:12	139
7:9-12	74, 95–96
7:12	22
8:5	81
14:1-4	124
21	54, 140
21:3	140
21:11, 23	54n5
21:12, 14	138
21:22	54n5
21:22-27	74
22:3-4	54n5
22:5	54n5

Subject index

Abihu, 6
Abraham, 73, 86
   God's promise to, 53
   worship by, 18
absolution, 85
achievement, 97
Adam and Eve, 60, 115
adoration, 5–6
   prayers of, 82
aesthetics, 110–114
   and music, 134–135
agape, 59
Ahio, 4
American Christians
   Evangelicals, praise and worship songs, 130
   religious freedom, 107
amplification system, 116
Ancient-Future Movement, xii
"And Can It Be" (Wesley and Campbell), 126
announcements, 62, 88–89
Anointing of the Sick, 98
"Anthem of Praise," 127
anxiety, 23
apostles, 74
Ark of the Covenant, 3–4
artists, 112
assertiveness, 98
authentic worship, 51, 100
   differences for individuals, 37
"awakened sinners," 70–71

Babel, tower of, 60
baptism, 27, 72–73, 98
beauty, 110–111
   problem measuring, 121
Beloved. *See also* Triune God
   impact on worshiper, 34–52
   love shaped by, 3–5
   loving response to, xiii
   preferences for worship, 15
   singing and love for, 127
Bible. *See* Scripture; *separate Scripture index*
biblical language, vs. psychological language, 104–105
biblical-typographical model, 8–9
   reasons for adopting, 9–10
Black Gospel music style, 131
"blended" corporate worship, 130
blessing, of Spirit, 29–30
body of Christ, baptism and, 72–73
Book of Common Prayer, 13
bride of Christ, 68–69

Cain and Abel, 24, 60
cardinal virtues, 46
cessationist position, 30–31
change, 98
charismatic spirituality, 30
Charlemagne, 90
children of immigrants, language for, 102
chosen people, 66–68, 95
   Triune God creation of, 119–120

Christ and Architecture (Bruggink and Droppers), 108
Christ-followers, 69, 70
Christian life, core, and love of God and neighbor, xiii
Christian Reformed Church in North America, xi
Christians, vocabulary of, 105
church, 27
    cessationist position and institutionalization of, 31
    as counter-cultural community, 105
    in New Testament, giving by, 87
    as people set apart, 54
    primary social task, 99
clapping, 88
cognitive approach to worship, 43
cognitive component of individual, 34, 36, 38
commands, to worship God, 23
communal rituals, 62
communication technologies, 116
communication with God, prayer as, 82
Communion. *See* Lord's Supper
community, 60
    adapting worship to, 99
    building, 62
    multicultural redeemed, 74–75
    visibility of, 68–72
complexity, in individual, 34–35
confession, 78, 83–85
    prayer of, 85
    as sacrament, 98
Confession of Belhar, 63
confirmation, 98
congregation, mission as, 55
congregational prayers, 62
congregational songs, 126
    diversity of, 75–76
conscience, examen of, 44
consciousness, examen of, 44
context of worship, 95–120
contextual worship practices, 100
Corinth, church in, 2
Cornerstone Knowledge, 108
corporate experience, baptism as, 73
corporate worship, 66
    arts in, 113
    "blended," 130
    as connected people, 55
    music in support of, 126
    as priority, 47
    space for, 106–110
    uniformity in, 51
counter-cultural worship practices, 101
courage, 46
creation, 115–116
    interaction with, 97
Creator, God as, 19
cross-cultural worship practices, 101
crosses in sanctuary, 109
cultural context, 96
culture, relationship to worship, 96–97, 99

David, 3–4, 18, 117
    praise from, 80
death, response to, 91
determination, 37
Diogenes, 82n16
directness, 98
discernment, viii
disciples, work of making, 95
discipline in worship, 78, 89–90
diversity, 73–76

Egypt, music in exodus from, 123
ekklesia, 66–67
El Salvador, 127
embodied person, worshiper as, 39–43
emotive component of individual, 34
    music and, 122
    in worship, 36
equality, 97
Ethiopian eunuch, baptism of, 73
Eucharist. *See* Lord's Supper
Eucharistic *ordo*, 9
examen, 44
experience, doctrine of Trinity and, 19
extended family, 67

faith, 45
family, 53–54
    extended, 67
fear, by worshipers, 24

SUBJECT INDEX

festivals, calendar of, 6
financial resources, for arts, 113
first-century Christians, songs of, 127
first day of week, significance, 89
forgiveness
    affirmation of, 85
    baptism as sign, 72

Garden of Eden, 115
gathered community, 66
    as mixed bag, 69–72
    space for, 106
Gathering-Word-Thanksgiving-Dismissal worship format, 13
generosity, 88
gifts, 86–89
    as expression of love, 117
    of Holy Spirit, 111
    for poor, 6
giving, 78
    sacrificial, 88
glory of God, 55
God
    grace of, 140, 141
    plan for heaven, 96
    self-giving, and our response, 14
God the Father, call to worship, 20–23
God the Son. *See also* Jesus
    as mediator, 23–26
God the Spirit. *See* Holy Spirit
Gospel, announcement of, 85
governments, hostility to faith, 106–107
grace, 26, 140, 141
gratitude, 86
    for saving grace in Christ, 22
"Great is the Lord," 127
"Great Is Thy Faithfulness," 128
Greatest Commandment, 57
grieving the Spirit, 28

Hannah, prayer, 80
happiness, 50
heart, 43–44
"heart language," 51, 101
heart of God, worship practices reflecting, 10
"heart style," of music, 131

Heidelberg Catechism, 54, 112
high priest, Jesus as, 25
High Tech Worship (Schultze), 116–119
holiness of God, 24
Holy Orders, 98
Holy Spirit
    body as temple, 44–46
    empowerment by, 2
    extra-ordinary gifts of, 29, 30
    gathered community as temple of, 28
    gifts of, 45
    power of, 45
    prayer to affirm, 31, 33
    promised presence of, 29
    role in worship, 10
    and singing, 124
    worship empowered by, 26–32
"Holy Spirit songs," 128
hope, 32, 45
host, of Sunday service, 67
"Hound of Heaven," 17
Houston, Whitney, 128
"How Great Thou Art" (Hine), 48, 128
human nature, art to tempt deficiencies, 113–114
humans
    bodies belonging to God, 42
    created for worship, 20–21
    in image of God, 21, 81
    need to worship, 23
    role in worship, 49
humility, 47
    physical position of, 85
    and praise, 80
hymns, 17, 80, 128
Hymns and Spiritual Songs (Watts), 128

"I Love the Lord," 127–128
"I Sought the Lord and Afterward I Knew," 17
image of God
    human beings in, 21, 81
    restrictions on portrayal, 112
    worship as person created in, 43–44
immigrant congregations, language for, 102–103
improvisational form of song, 129

individuality, 56, 97
informality, 97
institutionalization of church, cessationist position and, 31
institutions of culture, 98
international students, American values list for, 97
invocation, 31

Jerusalem, 86
Jesus, 6, 11
    as Bread of Life, 94
    on building Church, 67
    feet anointed with oil, 85
    Lamb of God, 138–139
    on love, 2, 59
    orientation of, 55
    prayer by, 62–63, 99
    redemptive work of, 21, 41
    as Savior of world, 74
John, 96, 138
Josiah, 18
joy, 47–48
judgment, refraining from passing, 71
justice, 46

Kedorlaomer (king), 86
The Knowledge of the Holy (Tozer), 79
Kyrie eleison, 129

Lamb of God, 138–139
language
    biblical vs. psychological, 104–105
    liturgical, 103–104
    similarities with music, 131
Last Rites, 98
latreia (worship), 13
leadership, gifts from Holy Spirit, 27
leitourgia, 11
LifeWay survey, 108
liturgy, 11–12, 47
    designing, 51
    language selection, 102
    love and, 62
    music selection principles, 134
    offering, 87
    and space design, 109
    with unison and responsive readings, 51
    vs. worship, 12
living sacrifice, 87
Lord's Day, and Sunday, 90
Lord's Supper, 91–94, 98
    frequency, 93
    preparation for, 64–65
    tables for, 109
love, 45
    formative power of, xii
    for God, 49, 50
    impact of, 86
    and liturgy, 62
    music and, 122
    neglecting gift of, 2
    by people of God, 57–62
    place in worship, 58–59
    technology and, 115–119
    and worship, xiii, 2
    worship as response, 3, 17–18
Lutheran World Federation, Study Team on Worship and Culture, 77

"Magnificat of the Old Testament," 80
manipulation, with music, 125
marriage, as sacrament, 98
Mary, 22, 80
mediator, God the Son as, 23–26
Melchizedek, tithe to, 86
memories
    love and, 91
    and music, 122
messages, from technology, 116–117
mid-week prayer meeting, 81
Miriam, 123
mission
    as congregation, 55
    of God, 53, 75
missional movement, 53
money, giving to God, 87
Moses, 18
motivation, 43
    to attend Sunday service, 71
multicultural redeemed community, 74–75
multigenerational worship, 62
music, 6, 88, 121–137

SUBJECT INDEX

aesthetics and, 134–135
for congregational worship, 76
diversity of congregational, 75–76
function of, 125–127
hymns, 17, 80, 128
language similarities with, 131
making it work today, 133–137
and memories, 122
power of, 124–125
prevalence of, 123–124
responsibility for selecting for worship, 134
singing, 123
styles of, 130–131
types, 127–130
musicians, space for, 106
mutual love, emphasis on, ix

Nadab, 6
Nairobi Statement on Worship and Culture Contemporary Challenges and Opportunities, 77–78, 100–101
Nebuchadnezzar, 123, 124
need, for worship, 23
New Covenant, 25
impact of, 6
New Jerusalem, 54, 140
New Testament, 9
and common space, 106
and local church, 67
New Testament church, giving by, 87
North Korean lullaby, 125

obedience, 6
Orthodox Christians, arts in worship, 112
Oxford Book of Prayer (Appleton), 83

patristic-ecumenical model, 8–9
patterns in culture, 98
Pentecostal movement, 30, 38
Pentecostal promise, 28
people of God, 55–57
mission as, 55
persecution, 107
personality types, 35
personhood, Cartesian definition of, 38

Pharisees, 82, 88
Jesus' conversation with, 85
Postman, Neil, 119
Power Failure: Christianity in the Culture of Technology (Borgmann), 117–118
power, of Holy Spirit, 45
practice, 78
vs. theory, xi
praise, 78, 79–81
as prayer, 82
praise and worship songs, 130
Praise-Proclamation-Recollection-Prayer worship format, 13
praxis-oriented regulative principle, 7–8
prayer, 19, 78, 81–83
to affirm Holy Spirit's presence, 31, 33
congregational, 62
Holy Spirit and, 29
with offering, 88
preparing, 83
types, 82
"Prayer for Illumination," 32
Prayer of Examen, 44
preparation, for worship, 42–43
Presbyterian Church (USA), xi
pretenders, 69–70
priest
believer as, 27
Jesus as high priest, 25
royal priesthood, 54n5
Principled Worship, xi
printing press, 116
priority, corporate worship as, 47
privacy, 97
professors of faith, 69–70
Prophets, 6
Protestant Christians
in 16th century, 7
arts in worship, 112
and emotive component, 38–39
life celebrations, 98
liturgical language, 103–104
prudence, 46
psalms, singing, 127

psychological language, vs. biblical language, 104–105
punishment, for failed worship, 23

qahal (Hebrew), 66–67

readings in liturgy, 51
recollection, 78, 90–94
reconciliation, 64, 84
Redeemer, God as, 19
Reformation, 37, 108
　sanctuary stripping, 112
Reformed Church in America, xi
regulative principle, 7–10
relationships, repair of, 64
resources, perspective on limited, 107
responsive readings, 51
righteousness, 46–47
rites, traditional, 98
rituals, communal, 62
Roman Catholics
　arts in worship, 112
　churches, 108
　sacraments, 98
royal priesthood, 54n5

sacraments, 98
Sacred Pathways (Thomas), 35–36
sacred space, God's preferences for, 106
sacrificial giving, 88
sacrifice, Jesus as, 24
St. John of the Cross, 28
Salem (Jerusalem), 86
sanctification, 46
　by praise, 81
sanctuary. *See* space for worship
sanctuary crosses, 109
Satan, 60
Saul, 123, 129
Scripture
　encounter with, 18
　music in, 121
　in vernacular, 101
　and worship, xii, 5–7
scripture songs, 129
Seeker-Sensitive Movement, xii
seekers
　music style for, 132

presence in worship, 71
transforming worshiper into, 84
and vocabulary, 104–105
self-centered approaches to worship, 23
self-interest, and worship, 49
self, seeing as God sees us, 84
selfishness, 50
service, worship as, 15
"Seven Stanzas at Easter" (Updike), 40–41
Simon (Pharisee), Jesus' conversation with, 85
sin, 21, 22
　awareness of, 24
　confession of, 83. *See also* confession
　divisive power of,, 63
　God the Spirit convicting, 28
　self-knowledge of, 44
singing, 123. *See also* music
Song of Deborah, 123
space for worship, 106–110
　consecration, 107
　resistance to change, 110
spectators, 56
Spirit of God. *See* Holy Spirit
Sunday, and Lord's Day, 90
Sunday service, 89
　host of, 67
　motivation to attend, 71
Sustainer, God as, 19

technology, 114–119
　description of, 116
　as means to worship, 118–119
television, 118
temperance, 46
Ten Commandments, 6
testimonies, 62
thanksgiving, prayers of, 82
Their Blood Cries Out (Marshall), 106–107
theological virtues, 46
theologically-oriented regulative principle, 8
theology, and sacred space, 109
theory, vs. practice, xi
thick worship practices, 78–79

praise as, 80
thin worship practices, 78
"Those Who Trust," 127
time, 97
tithe, 18, 86
tone of voice, ix
traditional rites, 98
transcultural worship practices, 77–78, 100
Triune God, 19–20
  balance in worship, 33
  hope for dynamic encounter with, 32
  loving response to, xiii
  mission of, 53
  and worship, 3, 5
  worship as response to love of, 140
Turner, Tina, "What's Love Got to Do with It?," 1

unbelievers, 70
unchurched Americans, church appearance preference, 108
Union Theological Seminary and Presbyterian School of Christian Education, xi
unity, affirmation of, 63
Uzzah, 4

vain glory, 82
vernacular language, Scripture in, 101
virtue, 46–50
visibility of people, 68–72
vocabulary, in worship, 103
volitional component of individual, 34, 36

war, 96
Wesley, John, 124–125
Westminster Confession, 8, 81

Westminster Shorter Catechism, 20, 55
white, American, suburban, Protestant (WASP) congregations, pursuit of diversity, 75–76
Word. *See* Scripture
Word-Sacrament worship format, 13
worship
  aspect of, xii
  cognitive approach to, 43
  considering new practice, 5
  constants in, 13
  context of, 95–120
  definition, 12–15
  essential components, 77
  gathering as family for, 56–57
  God's preferences for, 6–7
  inappropriateness of music styles, 132–133
  link with love, xiii, 2
  vs. liturgy, 12
  multigenerational, 62
  participation in, ix
  preparation for, 42–43
  reaction to diverse expressions of, 51
  relationship to culture, 96–97, 99
  as response to God's love, 3, 111
  as serious business, 6
  space, 106–110
  vocabulary in, 103
  and Word, 5–7
worship planners, 15–16
worship service. *See also* liturgy; Sunday service
  attendance, 89
worship wars, 60–61
Worship Wars (Long), 109
worthiness, 12–13

Zaccheus, 129
Zechariah, 11

www.ingramcontent.com/pod-product-compliance
Lightning Source LLC
Chambersburg PA
CBHW050816160426
43192CB00010B/1780